SWEET TALK

SWEET TALK

Sweeten Your Life with the Power of Your Words

"Pleasant words are as a honeycomb,
Sweet to the soul, and health to the bones."

Proverbs 16:24

Angela L Hill

Printed in the United States of America

First printing: 2024

ISBN: 979-8-218-53846-0

www.sweettalkbook.com

DEDICATION

"There is no greater agony than bearing an untold story inside you."

--Maya Angelou

This book is dedicated to all those that have ever had to sit through my long conversations, wondering why I talk so much, but continued to open their hearts, minds, and ears to me anyway.

It is through my spoken words that I have created a life that I love, and I thank you all for listening.

~ALH

TABLE OF CONTENTS

NOTE TO THE READER

When I decided to begin the first draft of this book, my mission was honest and simple: To share insight that would largely benefit those that would read it.

I've always harbored a deep love for books, and through the years, I've read more than I can count. But the books that truly capture my heart are the ones that whisper something new, the ones that resonate differently each time I pick them up. It's as if they have a life of their own, and every reading feels like catching up with an old friend with a new story to share.

My intention for this book is to craft chapters that not only capture your attention, but also linger in your mind, inviting constant reflection. I envision a book that's a perfect companion for your vacation, ideal for unwinding at night, and compelling enough to recommend to friends. Ideally, it will be engaging and worthy of revisiting often, rather than being a one-time read that gathers dust on a shelf.

As I poured my heartfelt thoughts into this book, I found myself, quite unexpectedly, uncovering new ways to heed my own advice. I began practicing a renewed version of this "sweet talk" that you'll soon learn about, and reminded myself how it felt to speak to my soul with a softer, sweeter tone. It was as if the words I wrote gently guided me to expand my own knowledge of what I thought I already knew.

As each paragraph formed first in my thoughts, then on paper, and finally into a typed manuscript, my own faith was deepened. The messages of affirmations, manifestation, visualization, intuition, movement, and just the pure love of life awakened something within me. I hope to bring you the same feelings of excitement and peace as you read this book.

Y'all ready?

♥

Most of us know that we are equipped with a whole mess of tools at birth, including our senses and natural instincts. Only when we are smart enough to tap into these precious gifts, can they be used to create the life we can only imagine (or so we think). The bible teaches us that God created man in His own image, both male and female, through His spoken word. Using his words, He blessed them. God saw all that He had made, and it was very good.

Through words that God spoke out loud, we became part of this infinite universe. Think about that for a second. God spoke the world into existence. Because of His words, we are living a human life and connected with one another here on earth. At the core of our being, our souls are full of love, hope, joy, and excitement. Since we were created in God's own image, we have the capability to love, create, innovate, and shape our world around us.

Amongst these valuable tools at our disposal as humans, is the practice of using our own words to create our environment. One example of this is our capacity to recite affirmations. Affirmations are the blessings that we speak over our lives. Think of them as reminders of who we are and who we are meant to be. They are our spoken words that affect the environment in which we live.

I frequently catch myself muttering words, or affirmations, during mundane chores, sometimes I boldly proclaim them when I'm tackling challenging tasks or projects (otherwise known as talking to myself!). Most of the time, I speak to myself in the sweetest, most genuine tone. Other times, I'm like a rigid teacher waving a wooden ruler, slipping into harsh statements that are purely used to push myself into gear!

Back in the day, (which could mean anytime between 10-40 years ago), I started to have serious talks with myself. We all do it, whether quietly inside our head or out loud. My talks turned into my own set of pep talks that I used to get through the day, like "You Got This" and "Think, Angela, Think." As I grew up, I began to recognize that some of these "pep talk" statements actually worked! I witnessed the concept of thoughts turning into things firsthand. I began tuning in to the way I talked to myself. What did my self-talk sound like?

We all have this inner voice, a self-talk habit, that we use to judge ourselves, guide our actions, and process our environment. I used to think I was crazy, muttering to myself like a psychopath! But it is the inner voice that we hear, and then goes on repeat like a broken record in our minds. This inner voice shapes our environment, influences our emotions, actions, and interactions with the world around us. We spend more time talking to ourselves than to anyone else, so shouldn't our self-talk be sweet talk?

Most often, my self-talk consisted of phrases such as "Why did you do that!" or "I need to do better." Usually, I criticized myself for my mistakes, or for not living up to my potential. As time went on, I really couldn't stand feeling "in trouble" or angry with myself all the time. This corruptive self-talk had me running in circles. I started to feel hesitant to take risks or to try new things. My self-worth began to dwindle, even though at my core I felt strong and courageous. How could I live a healthy life if I was always beating myself up and focusing on the negative? The number of times a day I spoke this way to myself was not only countless but now as I look back, it is also embarrassing.

One day, in a single transformative afternoon at a women's retreat, everything shifted for me. I realized how I had made it normal to constantly judge and berate myself. I discovered that the harsh self-talk was wounding my inner self, undermining my feelings of worthiness, confidence, and courage. I had been blaming myself for things out of my control and causing myself unnecessary pain for years.

On day two of this retreat, during a somber afternoon of reflection, I participated in a deeply impactful workshop that changed me forever. In a group setting, we were guided to begin a visualization exercise, forcing every attendee to break wildly out of their comfort zone. I remember vividly how I began to panic, (I absolutely hate these types of exercises), with fear just blatantly rising throughout every fiber of my being. I was committed to the outcome of this retreat, so I forced myself to participate fully to whatever was asked of me while I was there. After all, it was only four days long, and I was on a beautiful resort in Fort Lauderdale, Florida. Worst case, I could run out of the meeting room and spend the rest of my days on the beach!

But I knew my fear would lead to a breakthrough moment, so I pushed through.

In the group, with my eyes closed, I was instructed by the mentor to picture an early version of myself as a child and imagine her standing right in front of me. Conjuring up that image was easy, and I smiled as I visualized my cute little face.

Then, as the room fell silent, we were told to speak all of our self-talk directly to our younger selves. In my mind, we were face to face, and I spoke those hurtful self-judging words directly to her.

The pain and sorrow that washed over me were profound and overwhelming.

Experiencing this type of self-awareness was difficult, and the challenge was heightened by doing this exercise in a group setting with strangers. The room's piercing silence was only broken by the sounds of the other women crying, sobbing, and grappling with their own overwhelming guilt. This exercise didn't just alter my perspective; it compelled me to immediately change the way I spoke to myself internally.

What else did I learn from this experience? I recognized that words have intense power. I also saw evidence of myself instinctively cowering at my negative self-talk, instead of standing tall in all my worthiness in praise of my good traits.

It was as if a light bulb went off, connecting everything I had ever known about affirmations, to how our words form reality. In an instant, two separate beliefs were fused together to form a new picture in my mind. I finally understood and saw the effects of speaking negatively to myself, as well as out loud to others.

I wholeheartedly believed in the power of positive thinking and speaking. Yet, I didn't fully understand exactly how my words affected me until I was forced to pay attention to <u>how they made me feel</u>.

When we use God's toolbox to create our life experiences, we witness God's mercy and grace in our lives. Take a physical tool, like a hammer, for instance. We know how to use it, but there are thousands of uses for it that we haven't yet discovered. In this book, you're gonna learn how to sweet talk your way into the life you desire and most of all – deserve, using the tools we have been given in ways you may not yet understand.

Just as I discovered how to switch my thinking, you'll quickly find out that affirmations can become your best friend. Once you get the hang of it, you'll be proclaiming your words as blessings, rather than harsh judgements in no time.

The ins and outs of affirmations isn't considered rocket science, but it is science. However, there are no hard and fast rules for how you incorporate them into your life. Simply do what makes sense to you. I've learned a few things along the way about the practice of affirmations so I will share those tips with you.

Understand that affirmations are a personal reflection of your inner self, so take what resonates and just leave the rest.

I noticed that when I first started using affirmations, their impact was heightened when I concentrated on the words and focused on their meaning. When I spoke my affirmations on purpose, they resonated seamlessly with the energy I carried. In other words, when I paid attention to the purpose behind the words I used, I noticed their impact more quickly.

I also found that the more I spoke affirmations, the clearer and more precise the statements became. Whether it's during a daily routine, meditation, prayer, yoga, doing the dishes, walking dogs, or simply in quiet contemplation, practicing affirmations amplifies their effectiveness. And I want to share this creative practice with you.

Professing your faith in blessings and abundance out loud (or in your head) boosts their impact, and gives God, or the Universe, a message that you are ready to receive. It's as if you are giving yourself permission to be the person that you want to be. It's like putting a message in a bottle, or a note in a balloon, and sending it off to the powers that be, completely trusting you'll receive an answer.

Affirmations help you hone in to your authentic self. You begin to align with universal and divine powers that are waiting to grant you the opportunities you'll need to build the life you deserve. The work is to practice how to give the signal that you're ready to receive.

I've always been an outspoken, talkative person. I have never been afraid to make a new friend or talk to a stranger. My report cards always displayed that dreaded "C" in conduct and "talks too much" written in the comments. I participated in speech class, drama, debate, quiz bowl, cheer, dance, student council, and anything that satisfied my need to speak. I didn't care if anyone was listening. I used my voice to process my surroundings and my thoughts.

I've always thought of myself kind of like a sponge, just soaking up new ideas. I was constantly eager for educational opportunities to expand my knowledge on subjects of business, spirituality, and life in general. When I was in my 20's, I stumbled upon the art of Feng Shui. As a newlywed with a brand new house to decorate, I dove deep into understanding this philosophy. This horoscope-reading, moon-gazing, cloud-loving, God-praising girl began to connect the puzzle pieces of the science of our universe. It all started with learning about the effects of energy and sound on our environment.

I then broadened my curiosity to include all sorts of things like self-help, astrology, crystals, Bible study, prayer, and manifesting. I took in all this new information with a pinch of skepticism. You know, there are just so many "experts" out there teaching about these new age topics, and sorting through all that— it was quite a challenge. But it offered me a way to compartmentalize these larger-than-life thoughts I was thinking and the emotions that followed. I knew there was more to life than the reality I was being dealt, whether good or bad.

I yearned for success. I craved achievement. I loved to teach and share ideas with others. And checking off each line on my "to-do" list was and is still my favorite thing to do! I felt deep down that I was onto something special, something I'd always known about but couldn't quite put my finger on. As I explored further, I started to see the effects of my thoughts, actions, and ideas coming to life.

As I grew older, and a little bit wiser, I made it a point to surround myself with like-minded people. Sure, some friends and family thought I was a bit out there (and still do), but I was on a mission to shape my environment and design my own life. I had no idea how to begin, or if I was even doing anything right. But I stuck with it and found some of my favorite ways to find peace and navigate through this thing we call life.

Most of these classes, teachers, spiritual advisors, even therapists, all mentioned the subject of self-talk and positive thinking. But what does that really mean? I considered myself a positive thinker. I usually try to find the best in things. But I still found myself incomplete in fully understanding and applying the lessons I learned. Something was missing. The concept of finding the positive in everything seemed just very shallow. I felt determined to get to the heart of this seemingly superficial way to live.

At an early age, most of us are taught to sit in silence, listen to adults, and pray using the Bible. I learned the benefits and power of prayer from authentic Catholic nuns in school. They taught me how to pray for things, people, and circumstances. I found out that it's okay to speak victory over my life and my environment. In fact, it's expected. The bible says that **"Life and death lie in the power of the tongue" (Proverbs 18:21)**. The words that we speak aloud form our reality. How we think about ourselves, along with the way we speak to ourselves, have a profound effect on our life's circumstances. Positive words reinforce a hopeful mindset. Negative words are heavy and can weigh you down. Our thoughts we think and our words we speak can truly be a matter of life or death. They create positive or negative experiences. They evoke feelings of joy or despair.

Is it really possible to transform our lives simply by altering the words we think and speak?

Rewiring your mind (which is what it takes to change our thinking habits) doesn't come easily. While it's a straightforward process, it takes quite a bit of inner work. Anyone can simply repeat positive phrases and hope for the best. That's not what this book is about. Imagine a combination lock where every number must align perfectly to unlock it. I've aligned these chapters in a similar fashion: they connect seamlessly to unlock your true potential, and to show you the power you hold within to shape your world. Are you up for the challenge?

As I began to learn more and more about using affirmations, with each passing year I began to see signs of abundance. My blessings multiplied during the times I was most thankful. And I always remembered to wholeheartedly express sincere gratitude. But, I can't forget the times that I'd spontaneously speak words of thanks to God by literally looking up to the sky and announcing, "Thank You, God!" Blessings I'd prayed for, claimed victory over, and spoken out loud, started coming my way, quickly and unexpectedly, often in ways I couldn't quite explain. I knew it wasn't a coincidence, for there are no such things. I wondered how this was happening. How am I attracting the things and circumstances I just happen to think about, or that insignificantly crossed my mind? Many times, it was actual prayers that were answered, prayers that I had forgotten about ever praying. Other times it was deep desires requested from my heart or asked for out loud periodically during the day. Throughout this book, I'll be sharing some of these stories with you.

Ranging from the small to large, things started to work out for me as I learned about practicing affirmations, visualization, and intentional prayer...and so I started paying close attention.

Some days I just giggle when I think of these so-called "coincidences" that I know were born from my actual thoughts. I sit with silent silly smiles, or if it's crazy enough to really surprise me, I'll call someone right away to share my story. I even sometimes shake my head in disbelief, like this is insane. But I know it works for me. And it can work for you, too.

The way to speak affirmations is a personal and evolving practice. It requires some experimentation to find the right flow and discover what resonates with you as a unique human being. Some days, I focus solely on affirmations of gratitude, because that's what feels best to me. Other days, I might concentrate on thoughts of success or health. This process isn't exact or rigid, which is what makes it so valuable. You have the freedom to shape it in a way that feels right and benefits you!

Throughout these chapters, I'll use the phrase "Staying above the line". This idea refers to that unseen line between happiness/despair, joy/disappointment, excitement/depression.

We must choose to keep ourselves above that invisible line to truly soak in all the good fortune that comes our way. You'll hear me mention this term now and again throughout this book, and in detail in the chapter related to frequency.

Ultimately, my intention for this book is to help you start your own affirmation practice to attract more blessings into your life. Say as many as you want, or as little as you might need. Listen to your intuition - this isn't a list to just go through or recite as a task or chore. It's a starting point to a habit of verbally expressing your inner thoughts that will increase confidence, improve your well-being, and inspire action towards your goals.

Speak your affirmations, feel them, believe in them, and then let them go. The practice of letting go is a critical part of the formula. Let's say you're using an affirmation about wealth: *"Everyday, I attract money to me from all directions."* If you held on to that thought, eventually it would morph into a worry or concern about not having enough money! Your brain would convince you that you don't have money, you can't pay your bills, and you have no idea how money will come to you. This creates energy of lack, which is the opposite of what affirmations are intended to do!

I remember my MawMaw used to have a saying "A watched pot never boils." By speaking your affirmations aloud, letting them go, and changing your focus onto something else, you are allowing the energy of these positive words to go to work for you.

Affirmations are intended for you to speak as if you already believe in them. As if you already have what you desire and are speaking truth from the core of your being. You must believe to receive! This is not a practice of overthinking or rewriting. No begging. No speaking from a place of lack or want. It's like putting in your order at your favorite restaurant: *"I'll have a great day today with a side of good health."* Don't doubt your desires will come to you. Simply, let go of the thought and watch the magic happen.

Trust that the universe, God, your higher power, is aligning with your words to attract like a magnet everything you are declaring.

Throughout this book, I'll give you some general affirmations to help you get started. At the end of each chapter, use the empty page to write your personal affirmations, hopefully inspired by what you've read.

We can all become our best selves, and attract all that we deserve through inspiration, manifestation, listening to intuition, visualization, and declaring our abundance! Now, let's get into the details…

CHAPTER 1

Mastering Your Sweet Talk

"Do not let any unwholesome talk come out of your mouths, but only what is helpful for building others up according to their needs, that it may benefit those who listen."

Ephesians 4:29

Congratulations! You've taken the first step to learning how to sweet talk your way to your dream life. You are embarking on a beautiful journey of empowerment and transformation through the simple, yet powerful, practice of affirmations. I'm proud of you and ask that you be proud of yourself! Learning how to use affirmations and witnessing their positive effect can be a powerful force to incite change in your life.

So, you may be asking yourself, "What exactly are Affirmations?" The easiest way to explain them is: Affirmations are positive self-talk expressed through words, sentences, and phrases, spoken in a way that shifts your perspective on your surroundings.

1

Read that definition again. Notice the word "perspective." Affirmations aren't magic spells or hocus pocus. They are thoughts put into words, meant to **Shift - Your - Perspective**, which then attracts positive energy. This positive energy is the energy that created worlds. It is the Divine energy bestowed unto us that we use to shape our experiences and orchestrate our life circumstances.

Affirmations are as easy as talking to yourself, but with a focused and intentional purpose. In my experience, they are a necessary part of attracting good things into your life. Affirmations work to align your energy with positive vibes. They can also help shift your mood from negative to positive, which is useful in reframing your mind's perspective. They don't have to be complex phrases or heavily thought-out sentences. They are the simplest forms of words formed in your mind that AFFIRM good thoughts, clever ideas, positive feelings, and healthy viewpoints.

Affirmations can be used anytime, anywhere, and as I'm gently reminded on a daily basis, they often help shake off negative vibes when you're feeling blah. I know many people who use affirmations to soothe themselves during life's toughest challenges. Sometimes we need something, anything, to just calm us down, and help us get through fear, or confusion.

We all have been down that broken road where something sets us off and we start to spiral. We've experienced a time when negative thoughts came flooding in, and we somehow lost all sense of control. The more you practice using affirmations to slow that momentum, the easier it becomes to stop yourself from spiraling downward.

When I recently went through an extensive job search, I had to put this advice into practice. Rejection after rejection really began taking me down a notch. Each time I'd check my email, it seemed to get more difficult to remain positive. I'd find myself drifting into a negative mind space, and the downward spiral was a constant struggle.

One morning, I realized I was tired of being tired. I knew in my heart that I was experiencing a temporary situation. I remembered that things always work out for me, and I became determined to shake off the bad mood, depressing thoughts, and negative perspective. Then and there, I made a conscious decision to not let those negative thoughts drag me down. I forced myself to take a moment, shut my computer, and open my mind to affirmations to try and lift myself back up. I like to think my affirmations during those times were my true spirit talking to me. Like a best friend through internal dialogue, talking me out of panic and anxiety, and into acceptance and peace.

"Things are always working out for me."

"This is temporary."

"I trust in my abilities to secure a job that's a perfect match to me."

"The perfect job is on its way to me."

"I trust God's plan for me."

"My next chapter is on its way and it is amazing."

"I am so grateful for the opportunity to attract a new job that fits me perfectly."

When you work on being strong enough to resist a knee-jerk, negative reaction to your environment, you keep your power. You also strengthen your "energy" muscles, teaching yourself to stay in a high frequency vibe. When you live in a positive, good energy vibe, you begin to attract the good things meant for you.

Even if you start slowly, by just stating the obvious *"This feels like it sucks but it is temporary"*, and work your way up to *"I am willing to believe that things always work out, even when they don't feel like it"*, you'll start to feel better. A subtle soothing of your emotions.

My Great Aunt Mamie used to say *"That ain't nothin'"* whenever things would go sour, to remind us that our problems don't always have to consume us. Sometimes it's difficult to jump

4

from negative straight into the positive, so allow yourself some space to slowly make that transition with affirmations.

Soothing ourselves is an important benefit of speaking affirmations. My dog, Cooper, is known for his anxiety and weird behaviors. One of his habits is soothing himself by biting into a pillow while closing his eyes. This is his method for managing the intense emotions of his current situation like loud noises or over-stimulation. My house guests think this is rather weird, but I get him. It's his version of a 'time out' for him to stop and reset his mind. We can use affirmations to reset our brains and shift the focus away from those negative situations our thoughts just love to cling to.

Included in the basic concept of practicing affirmations is the unfaltering belief that <u>Words Become Reality</u>. When we tell our story, our story becomes our reality.

What's your story? Is it negative self-talk? Is it fear based? Are you thinking those thoughts now? "This book isn't going to help me", "This stuff is all made-up", "I'll never be able to change my thoughts", "My life is just what it is and will always be", "Things are hard for me, I'll never change my point of view". Is that the story you want to tell? Stop telling the story of defeat, anger, depression, hardships and start telling the story of success, happiness, blessings, and abundance!

I notice that when I wake up "on the wrong side of the bed," my day sucks. It becomes one hardship after another and at the end of the day I'm just glad it's over. Do I want to live like that? NO! I used to give up and think the day was spoiled from the start. But that just perpetuated the cycle to continue. The use of affirmations helps me turn my circumstances around the moment I recognize I'm falling into a negative thought pattern.

We CAN create our life - we CHOOSE to feel a certain way about our circumstances. Shouldn't we at least learn how to choose happiness and hope instead of sadness and despair?

Our moods can flip in the blink of an eye. Ever noticed how a toddler can go from a full-blown tantrum to giggles and grins just by diverting their attention to something delightful? It's a quick shift, much like how we can change our own moods with a simple change of focus. We can choose how we want to feel at every moment. When someone disagrees with you, you can argue, feel threatened, angry, bitter. Or you can just agree to disagree or respect their perspective, and quickly change the subject. You can let the disagreement fester, continue bringing it up to your friends, talk about injustice, and allow your mind to swirl with all the ways things aren't "fair" to you.

Or you can choose to move on from it on a new day with a new story. It's all a choice.

Easier said than done, right? Yep, I know. But working through the process of affirmations will shift your state of being to automatically stop caring about all those trivial things. You'll begin to crave the feeling of happiness, worthiness, joy, excitement, anticipation. Since you'll be busy declaring abundance and prosperity - you won't have time to let those negative things bother you anymore.

Slowly, you start to give up on the idea of controlling others, and you no longer care about being right. Your feelings, your true sense of self, becomes stronger, and stands up to the bully inside of you that judges and wants to fuss at you all the time.

You will begin to recognize when you are allowing your mind to push you to speak negative thoughts out loud. You will feel the discord between those negative words and your actual inner self that craves peace and joy. The quicker you change focus, the faster you begin to feel better, which makes it easier to attract better circumstances for your life.

Many scientists and spiritual seekers have long known about the concept of words becoming reality. Thousands of books have been written and hundreds of speeches and presentations given on the subject. Some doctors, scientists, and spiritualists have produced studies and research papers, ranging from the simple ideas to the complex. Chances are you've known about this for a long time and filed it away in the back of your mind, until now. Now is when you are receptive to understanding it. It's like when you listen to a heartbreak song over and over, and it never really 'hits' until you are experiencing heartbreak? Then you say to yourself "Ohhhh, I get it now!" As the old saying goes – "The teacher appears when the pupil is ready."

Our lives play out in a series of lessons. Sometimes, we can't skip lessons or jump too far ahead. Do you ever get the feeling that you have the answer, or the solution to a problem, but it's just slightly out of reach? That's because there is more to be revealed. Something more that you need to learn in preparation for that particular stage of life. Affirmations open our minds to help us through the dark tunnels with ease. They assist with keeping our mind focused on the good, so with gratitude and eagerness, we can face each chapter as it appears to us.

When you speak thoughts out loud, you give them life. You make them real. You create their energy, and they become a vibration. This vibration echoes into the universe, attracting similar energies (positive or negative), manifesting your thoughts into tangible outcomes. God hears them, the Universe feels them. Your body reacts to them. Each word professed out loud sparks an idea, a feeling, a breath of something soon to become.

Any words or phrases that help you to rewire and refocus your brain on the positive are considered affirmations. Any word or phrase you speak can manifest into reality, so choose them wisely. Each person has their own way of practicing affirmations. The catch is - they aren't "wishes" or empty promises made to yourself. They aren't prayers, although God is always listening. They are more like pep-talks, spoken in small doses, which provide motivation throughout your day. Think of affirmations as building blocks, or bricks, which are being fused together one by one to build the life you desire. They are intentional statements, and they can - and will - have a profound effect on your circumstances.

Odds are, you're already speaking affirmations, probably not intentionally, and most likely not realizing it. *"I can do this!"* Is a great example of a useful affirmation. *"I got this!"* and *"I can figure this out!"* are examples of the whispers (or screams) that we may speak to ourselves to get through rough patches, and to also attract positive energy to our space. "I am" statements are my absolute favorite. They give your spirit life, reframe your health, mind, and body.

"I am healthy."

"I am designing the life I want."

"I am inviting money to all parts of my life."

9

"I am allowed to move past people things that no longer serve me."

"I am creating a life of abundance and joy."

If you want to begin seeing your life pivot towards the life you desire, start with these types of affirmations.

On the flip side, speaking negative affirmations, whether you realize you do this or not, will keep you stuck. Stuck in confusion, negative feelings, maybe even depression. "I'll never get out of this mess," "I'll never be good enough." Whenever you speak these thoughts, you are giving them life, and keeping yourself surrounded by a negative perspective. There is power in your tongue. Stop talking about how you're tired, exhausted, broke, angry, frustrated, and incomplete. These thoughts create blockages that keep you from experiencing all the blessings meant for you.

Shifting unhealthy words to encouraging statements will move you towards the practice of faith, belief, love, and prosperity. Sometimes we speak negatively without realizing it. It's a sign of a bad habit to break, and we all have our share of bad habits. Begin by recognizing your negative thoughts, then force yourself to remain quiet. Don't speak them out loud. Instead, think of how you can replace them with different statements:

"This problem will pass quickly."

"I am attracting solutions at every turn."

"I know better days are ahead."

"I trust the journey of my life."

Start by speaking your vision out loud. With each sentence, purposely visualize your statements, and take a moment to experience the positive energy that each improved thought brings.

Ok, this sounds great, right? But if you've never intentionally spoken affirmations before, where do you begin?

From start to finish in this book, as you learn about how affirmations can help you build a life filled with abundance, I will sprinkle suggested affirmations throughout and at the conclusion of each chapter. Use these generic affirmations as a starting point and as inspiration. But, by the time you finish reading this book, my hope is that you'll have created your own personal affirmations that really speak to you and resonate with you. The general affirmations throughout each chapter are offered as guidance and are designed to be simple to articulate. Don't worry, they are a great foundation. If all you can do is repeat the ones I provide in this book, that is enough, and can lead to the outcomes you seek. Frequently, they will evolve into a version that is uniquely yours, so don't give up!

The best way to kickstart this journey of sweet talkin' your way through life is to choose words and phrases that resonate with your inner spirit, then embrace consistent repetition. This isn't a complicated process. Simply use your existing ways of speaking to your advantage. This book will help you do it with intention and focus, which is what works!

Every now and then, you might come across a word or phrase that just doesn't sit right with you, whether you're whispering it to yourself or saying it out loud. This is what I mean by "resonating with your inner spirit." We'll dive into this deeper in the chapter on Intuition. But as an example, let's say you want a new house. Speaking *"I am grateful I am attracting my new house"* may not feel as good as *"I have everything I need to find the best house for me."* The statement *"I love knowing the perfect house will find me,"* and *"I appreciate my job that earns me a salary for my new house"* might feel more comfortable. Can you tell the difference? Affirming that you have the guidance and tools necessary to reach your goals sometimes feels better than acting as if you have them. This is an effective way to begin, until you get comfortable rising to the frequency and feeling worthy to claim all that you deserve.

Taking a slight step back in expressing your needs in your journey helps to frame your affirmations in the way that your brain and spirit can accept.

Remember, you must 100% BELIEVE in the affirmations, so take small steps, if need be, as long as you have 100% faith in them. God knows if you're lying, and the universe will react to your feeling and emotions more than the words. In other words, if you are thinking "This is never gonna work" while you repeat the phrase "*I am abundant*," you'll give up after some time because the energy matched your feelings instead of your words, and nothing will ever change.

Do you ever feel stuck even though you have happiness and direction in your life? Not being aligned with your thoughts causes you to be stuck and confused. If you don't believe you deserve your blessings, you'll feel off-kilter. Speak smaller affirmations that are easier to believe.

"I have everything I need to succeed."

"I am growing richer every day."

"Good things are always happening to me."

Once you settle on the words and phrases that resonate with you, write them down or memorize them so that you can repeat them as needed. Repetition is the heartbeat of effective affirmations. Think of it as watering seeds in the garden of your mind. The more you repeat an affirmation, the deeper its roots grow, anchoring it firmly in your subconscious. This consistent repetition creates a habit, reinforces positive thought patterns, and gradually reshapes your beliefs and attitudes.

Repeat! Repeat! Repeat! Establish a daily routine for speaking your affirmations. Open your heart to speaking them whenever they cross your mind, but also at specific times. Whether it's during your morning shower, daily commute, or before bedtime, notice a time that suits you best, and stick to a schedule. Consistency is key, so make it a habit, like brushing your teeth or having a cup of coffee. Then, choose your favorite affirmations to sprinkle throughout the day, but stay consistent on your focused affirmation ritual.

The moment you open your eyes in the morning is a wonderful way to start your day with a pleasant outlook and positive phrase. *"Today is a good day."* Do it before your mind even realizes what's happening. We all have digital technology - so use your iphone, Alexa, Siri, TV, Radio, whatever is at your disposal, to remind you to say your affirmations. If you don't have technology, use notes to remind you. I have my Alexa set to play the song "This is the Day the Lord Has Made" at 9am each day. Some days, it seems like a nuisance! But each time it begins to play, I remind myself that I am setting the tone for the day and *"I am going to have a great day!"* Do whatever it takes to create a routine that incorporates your affirmations.

14

Speak your affirmations loud and heartfelt! I'm so confident when I say my affirmations, even my dogs sit up and listen, thinking I'm giving them commands. When I declare blessings over my day, I sometimes use the term "We" so they can enjoy them too! It also helps me to create the habit. In the morning, I speak these words out loud:

"We are going to have a great day!"

"We are safe!"

"We are loved!"

I especially use affirmations when I am frazzled, to reframe my state of mind, for instance when the dogs are misbehaving. *"I am so thankful to have you as a best friend to keep me company"* instead of "Why did I adopt these dirty dogs." See what I did there? Instantly, I look at their smiling faces, muddy paws, tongues hanging out, and think *"Wow, I really do love having you around."*

As you take your first sip of coffee, whether you're perched at your kitchen table, settled into your favorite chair, inside or out on the porch, or even in your car on the way to work, take a moment to truly enjoy that first delightful taste. Think thoughts like:

"I am so thankful for this coffee."

"This is delicious coffee."

"This coffee feels amazing to drink and my day is going to be fantastic."

"Everyday my life gets better and better."

Speak these thoughts out loud. It's a breeze to slip affirmations into each part of your day. It is as simple as deliberate positive thinking. A "slowing down" if you will, to savor each moment of goodness and blessings.

When you find yourself in a time of gratitude, joy, and positivity, do your best to drag out the feeling. Make it last. Make a conscious effort to enjoy the good vibes for as long as you can. The longer you keep yourself surrounded by positive energy, the stronger it becomes, and the better chance that feeling will stay with you throughout the day. These small, indistinctive positive moments are what matters in life. The more we engage with good, positive energy, the more an imaginary bubble forms around us, protecting us from the negative energies of the day. A momentum begins - keeping us on the positive train all day long!

Now, before you think "This is stupid," (which I have heard from lots of people when I tell them stories of how I received blessings from practicing affirmations), I'm going to use the old saying - Don't Knock It Till You Try It!

I choose to believe that you are here for a reason. You picked up this book because you were either searching for this message or you were intuitively guided to read it. Even if I was the one who handed you this book, it's your own energy that drew its message to you. You see, that's the beauty of this practice - you don't have to second guess or doubt because what you attract WILL reach you, no matter how or when. No matter how big or small. With each chapter, you'll gain a deeper understanding of energy and the part it plays in your life.

Don't just think and say your affirmations—go ahead and jot them down on paper. The act of physically engaging with your words by writing each word reinforces the message. Some people enjoy keeping a journal just for affirmations, letting you track your progress, remember the best ones, and mark your favorites. Use whatever you have handy - my favorite is sticky notes and oh, so many notebooks! What God puts in your mind and soul to be or do, isn't an accident. It is meant for us to acknowledge these thoughts of how we want our life to be. It isn't enough to just hope for happiness. Writing down your hopes and desires makes them concrete, like facts. It's also a good trick to remind you to speak them each time you see your written notes. Every chance you have to read your affirmations is another chance to get that uplifting energy moving to create positive circumstances.

I have several colors of sticky notes, various notebooks and notepads, and even use the notes section in my phone to jot down my affirmations. I've used fancy pens, colored pens and pencils, and doodled art around my words to stay focused and creative. You can put notes on your desk at work, in your car, on your refrigerator, and anywhere you want to be reminded of the power of your affirmations. I have them on my light switches, my nightstand, my computer, even in desk drawers. Don't worry if people see them! You'll be amazed how quickly the energy in the room shifts, when your affirmations light up the souls that read them.

Allow the feeling and emotion of the affirmation to direct your writing. Write your greatest desires in the form of affirmations.

"I am a millionaire."

"I am abundant."

"My life is blessed by God."

"I am attracting the perfect partner."

"I attract good things with ease and grace."

"Everyday I am getting healthier and wealthier."

Write down whatever you need to be reminded of during your day. You could write your love affirmations in red, money affirmations in green, and so on. Whatever works for you is going to work for you!

When you take the time to write down your affirmations, it's like you are signing a contract with the universe, to bring forth everything you desire. It is "inking" your affirmation. Not to mention, when you walk around your desk or home and see all these positive words and phrases, you can't help but feel like you are attracting good things to your life.

"I am successful."

"I am attracting good things in my life with ease."

"My life feels wonderful."

In the Bible, there is a scripture that is often referred to as encouragement for writing down goals and aspirations as a step towards making them a reality. It asks us to record the vision clearly and plainly so that it can be acted upon.

"Then the LORD answered me and said: 'Write the vision and make it plain on tablets, that he may run who reads it." (Habakkuk 2:2)

When you begin speaking victory over your life, you start to inspire others with your faith, joy, and positive energy. You start attracting other people that have similar views and perspectives, and it starts a snowball effect. The abundant energy expands outward, and everyone reaps the rewards of your sweet affirmation phrases.

When I packed up and moved to a new city for a new job, I was thrilled to be handed a blank page to start writing a new chapter of my life exactly how I wanted it to be. On my very first day, a colleague said to me: "I manifested you into my life." Those were her exact words to me, bless her sweet heart. That was day one, and she was the first soul I bumped into in this new town. She was convinced that our energies aligned, and of course, we became friends. I took to her right away, like a bee to honey—we were fast friends from the get-go.

"Thank you for allowing other like-minded souls to cross my path."

"I attract wonderful people into my life with ease."

Life doesn't unfold on accident, and the people that are meant to be in your world will just show up. Every soul you meet has something to teach you or a bit of joy to add to your journey.

One particular morning, I had this gut feeling about my friend, like something significant had happened over the weekend. I was just about to call her, but she beat me to it. The moment I answered her call, the first words out of her mouth were "I'm a millionaire." I immediately responded, "Of course you are!" She instantly sent me photos of her sticky notes that read "I am a millionaire" and "Millionaire pending…I am wealthy."

And the last photo was of her winning lottery ticket.

Was she lucky? Nope.

Did she create this on purpose? Yep!

You see, she never doubted. Even when I would fall below the line, meaning when I fell into a negative thought pattern - she would pick me up and say "No, no, no, we don't do that." She was a true inspiration of how to remain positive, live your life as if God himself is standing next to you (which he is), and declare blessings and victory upon your life. Her jackpot lottery win was no accident. She created this for herself.

She attracted what she believed she deserved.

You see, when practicing affirmations, it is mandatory to cultivate an unwavering belief. You must Believe to Receive! Belief is the fuel that propels affirmations from mere words to life-altering tools. To maximize their impact, you must cultivate unwavering belief in the truth of your affirmations. Unshakeable Faith. This requires a shift in perception, accepting that positive change is not only possible but inevitable.

We all have this capacity. Abundance and wealth aren't just for some and not others. The difference between my friend and most of us is that she KNEW beyond a shadow of a doubt, that she was going to be a millionaire. She surrounded herself with other like-minded people, listened to her intuition when she made decisions, and remained humble at every turn. When things would go wrong, she would simply state "Not today, I know I'm blessed and meant for bigger and better things."

As you can imagine, it takes working daily to brush aside negative thoughts or images that enter your mind as you repeat your affirmations. Friends, this is a minute-by-minute, day-by-day practice. If negative thoughts arise, train yourself to refocus on your positive affirmations. Turn them around. Memorize a few that can help you such as *"I am safe"* or *"Things are always working out of me."* These will eventually become second nature when fear and doubt try to enter your mind, and they will support you in turning toward the direction that you want to go.

"I allow negative thoughts and emotions to flow far from me like a river."

"I let go of all things not meant for me."

"I invite peace and abundance into my life."

When I first dipped my toes into the practice of affirmations, I'd pore over the words written by others and echo them back, just like learning a new recipe from an old cookbook. Some were lengthy, some I'd forget as quickly as I'd read them. It took me some time to realize that we need to choose affirmations that resonate with us on a personal level. They should feel authentic and align with our individual core values. The more relatable and believable the affirmations, the easier it is for your mind to accept and internalize them. Reword them into the language you speak and the way you would normally say them. Use everyday words to resonate with your mind. For instance, if you want to use the word "transformation" but the synonym "change" feels better to you, then by all means use it. It's not just the words but the intent that is going to bring the results you want.

Remember, small steps forward are just as good as giant leaps. If you feel it's too big of a jump to truly believe "I'm a millionaire!", try softer variations such as:

"I have everything I need."

"I'm abundant and the universe always provides for me."

"I am healthy and wealthy."

"I am always on the right path."

Take the instance of my friend, who said *"I'm a millionaire pending."* She was convinced it was on its way, and that statement felt more closely aligned with what she believed.

These smaller, more believable, affirmations help reframe your mind to accept the good in the present, rather than your mind struggling to believe something that, deep down inside, isn't actually true (yet). This type of inauthentic thought will only lead to frustration and doubt, which is the opposite of what we are trying to do.

The goal is for your words to feel easy, peaceful, and true, void of any contrasting thought or feeling.

When you phrase your affirmations in the present tense, it is if they are already true. This is a big deal in the practice of affirmations and manifestation. Instead of saying, "I will be confident," say, "*I AM confident.*" This small shift is important for your mind to accept the affirmation as a current reality, reinforcing your belief in its truth. By speaking in present terms, it is as if you already have it, not that you are wanting it. It represents a pattern of abundance, instead of one of lack. Speaking in the present tense is critical. Acting as if it is you already have it, you condition your mind to actually believe it. Attracting the energy of abundance generates clarity on the actions you'll take to make it a reality.

In the instance of my millionaire friend, notice she didn't proclaim "I WILL BE a millionaire", but instead "Millionaire pending." See the difference? Slight change but a huge energy shift.

Allow your affirmations to adapt and grow with you as your circumstances and goals evolve. They're meant to be flexible and move with your circumstances. If you've ever had the pleasure of watching magnolias in full bloom swaying in the breeze as a summer storm starts to brew, you get what I'm saying. This flexibility ensures that your affirmations are always relevant and supportive, reflecting your current needs and goals at any moment.

As you evolve, so should your affirmations, transforming them into a dynamic tool for navigating the various stages and phases of life.

The moment my daughter got engaged, I began using affirmations to set up the experience, the process, and the wedding day. I announced every day *"This wedding is as perfect as it can be."* When she chose an outdoor wedding in the month of September, I had my doubts. They sure do creep in quickly, don't they? As sure as a mosquito bites your leg on the bayous of Louisiana, the fear of stormy weather came rushing in. So, what did I do?

I began my wedding affirmations, of course!

"I have everything to prepare for the perfect wedding."

"This wedding is a dream come true."

"The weather is clear, beautiful, and I thank you God for preparing a gorgeous day for us."

"I trust that things are always working out for me."

Then...two days before the wedding, Hurricane Francine arrived.

My home was right smack in its path, and we were without power for an entire day. I leaned into my affirmations so hard and fierce that the storm swept in and out in just a day, leaving no damage behind. I pulled out every tool from my proverbial toolbox

25

to affirm the perfect wedding day. And you know what? The weather turned out simply gorgeous. Perfect, I tell you. And would you believe it? The very minute, the exact second the last guest stepped into the reception hall, the skies just opened up and it poured! It felt like God Himself was holding off the rain just for us. So many things came together that day to make it perfect, and I know deep down I played a part in making that happen.

"Things are always working out for me."

Before you dismiss the idea, let me be clear: I'm not suggesting that you can single-handedly control a storm, disease, death, or other life events that might be part of God's plan. Instead, I believe we have the opportunity to rise above certain challenges that aren't necessarily meant for us. Here on earth, we possess free will and the creative power to shape our realities and walk alongside God. The wedding choices that were made, all the way from choosing this town I would live in, to selecting a venue, and setting the wedding date, led us down the path to what turned out to be the perfect wedding day.

As your journey unfolds, you'll find yourself refining and adapting your affirmations to match your growth. Gratitude will take root, and the thrill of using affirmations will further fuel the manifestations that spring from them. Excitement and anticipation are proof that you are serious about getting results. These feelings generate a feeling of expectation, and the universe must answer.

Ultimately, this is what we are all searching for: Excitement. Anticipation. Eagerness. Happiness can be overrated - what is happiness, anyway? Happiness is merely a fleeting reaction to an external circumstance. Joy is a deep feeling of pleasure that is more enduring and profound than momentary happiness. Excitement, joy, and eagerness light that fire within us that makes us passionate about life. That's what gets us up in the morning. That's what keeps us going during the day and pushes us to survive the hard times we must endure. We can believe we are enough, but the thrill to evolve into a better, authentic self is where the magic lies.

Have you ever had the thought *"What if everything works out perfectly?"* These kinds of thoughts keep the spark of anticipation and enthusiasm burning, fueling our motivation every single minute of the day. Sometimes, we're searching for an answer. When one isn't easy to come by, it can ruffle our feathers and make us frustrated. But asking yourself these questions is a form of affirmations, and it sure does help soothe your spirit, guiding you toward a better feeling thought.

Once you climb up to feelings of anticipation, eagerness, and wonder, truly immerse yourself in them. You don't have to tame your feelings. Let them flow freely and savor every bit of the positive energy they bring.

Don't let one good thing satisfy you. Keep speaking victory over your life, keep the sweet talk flowing. Don't stand still. Win a million dollars? Ask for two. Alter your affirmations to *"I am a multi-millionaire!"* Nothing is too big or too small. Expect results. Imagine how you will feel when your highest goal is reached. Keep that feeling throughout the day.

Turn your thoughts and affirmation notes into a picture in your mind. Imagine it like a beautiful painting or a cozy quilt, stitched together with all your hopes, dreams, and positive words. Let that image be as clear and vibrant as the sun in the sky, guiding you toward the life you want to create. We all daydream - make your daydreams count!

Positive visualization acts as the bridge between your affirmations and the reality you wish to create. By vividly imagining the desired outcome while reciting affirmations, you amplify their impact and send a clear message to your subconscious mind. You evoke feelings, emotions, and vivid details to your mind as if you already have health, wealth, happiness, and success. They have no choice but to now appear before you. We will dive deeper into visualization in a later chapter.

It's simple to close your eyes and clearly visualize the positive outcomes that come with your affirmations. Engage your senses—feel the emotions, see the details, and hear the sounds. This visualization process enhances the emotional connection to your affirmations. Picture yourself having everything you want and need. Visualize each step you'll encounter as you progress through every phase of achievement. The journey matters. Focus on each step you take and recite the affirmations that support your goals.

Sometimes, creating a vision board that visually captures your affirmations can really be a game-changer. It's like putting all your vibes and dreams right there on your wall, which can help keep you motivated and on track with your goals. It's like having a constant reminder of where you're headed and what you're manifesting into your life. A vision board is a powerful and creative tool used to visually represent your goals, aspirations, and desired outcomes, especially if you are a visual person. It serves as a tangible tool that brings your thoughts into reality. Collect images, quotes, and symbols that align with the actions aligned with achieving your goals. Place the vision board in a prominent location where you'll see it daily, serving as a constant reminder of your aspirations. There are hundreds of blogs and Pinterest boards with tips and advice on creating vision boards. If this seems interesting to you, I'd recommend trying it out, using some ideas you can find easily on the internet.

As you embrace the power of repetition, belief, and positive visualization, you embark on a journey of self-discovery and empowerment.

The words you choose to speak today have the power to shape the reality you live tomorrow.

Remember that your affirmations are personal to you. Each of us has our own unique set of affirmations that resonate and work for us. You will find that speaking certain affirmations affect your mood, energy, and your daily life. What works for you may not work or even make sense to others. So be sure to stay flexible, like a willow tree swayin' in the breeze, as you go about discovering which affirmations make you feel all positive and vibrant. It's all about finding those sweet words that light you up inside and make your heart sing.

My affirmations change from day to day, but each and every day, I make sure to say the ones listed below. They are easy to remember and roll right off the tongue. I find they always work for me and improve my mood and circumstances.

"Things are always working out for me."

"I have everything I need, and the universe supports me."

"I am connected to the divine energy that flows through me."

"I'm exactly where I'm meant to be."

"I attract positive energy and new opportunities into my life."

"I am grateful for the opportunities that come my way."

"I am surrounded by abundance."

"I am loved."

"I am safe."

"I feel at peace."

"I have the power to create my own experiences."

"I receive everything I need in perfect, divine timing."

"I grow healthier and wealthier every day."

Be open to speaking the words that work best for you.

MY AFFIRMATIONS WORKSHEET

CHAPTER 2

Finding Your Way Through Intuition

"And your ears shall hear a word behind you saying, 'This is the way, walk in it,' when you turn to the right, or when you turn to the left."

Isaiah 30:2

In the center of a stressful time in my life, I bought a house sight unseen, 500 miles away in another state. Can you believe that? My intuition is usually spot on, and I trusted it to guide my decision to purchase a new home. Well, if I'm being honest, I also trusted friends and family to check it out for me, but the true test was "Did it FEEL right to me?" Yes, it most certainly did. You can say that I was sure as the okra in my gumbo I had called the perfect home into my life—the very one I prayed for, spoke my affirmations over, and expected to appear.

I am known as an avid overthinker, (most Virgos are!). I like to make plans, I <u>need</u> to know every detail, and surprises are the enemy to me. Practicing the art of letting go and allowing my inner guidance to be my guide has been a long and turbulent process. I fought with myself often. I had to learn how to heed my own advice without talking myself out of one thing or another. Until one decision based on intuition worked out, and then another, and then another. I eventually learned how to listen to, and obey, my intuition. And boy, did those blessing start flowing in!

I'm the girl that would make plans based on my intuition, and then allow my brain to force me to cancel said plans. Some people called me wishy-washy. Or told me I wasn't good at making decisions. The truth is, I was great at making decisions, but I was just terrible at second-guessing myself all because of those deep-rooted limiting beliefs (plus an overactive Virgo brain).

A few years before I headed up to Nashville, I was living in Baton Rouge, right around the time Garth Brooks was putting on a show at Tiger Stadium. It was a huge event, and my intuition told me to buy tickets. How could I miss hearing *"Calling Baton Rouge"* in the most exciting stadium around? Something inside was tugging at me to go to that concert, like a persistent friend who won't take no for an answer. I ignored these inner messages for months until the day of the concert arrived.

I had no tickets. For all I knew, they were sold out. I had no one to go with. Most of my friends were already there. But no matter how hard I tried, I just couldn't ignore my inner voice pushing me to get to that stadium. Finally, I called my daughter, she rounded up some friends, grabbed last minute tickets on an app, and bam, just like that, we were going to the concert.

Suddenly, I felt sick to my stomach. As I was getting ready, my Virgo brain was in a state of horror. How can you go to a concert without planning? Where will you park? Where are your seats? How long will it take for us to get there? What if we are late? What if we are stuck in traffic? What am I going to wear? You know, just those usual negative thoughts your brain throws at you to talk you out of being spontaneous and obeying your intuition.

I took a few deep breaths, whispered some affirmations to myself, and decided to go to that concert on this crazy whim, planning be darned.

"I can do this."

"This is an opportunity I want to pursue."

"Thank you for giving me the chance to go to this concert!"

Our seats were in the nosebleed section, at the very top of the open roof stadium, so high I had to take a break halfway up my climb to the top. Maybe my concert seats weren't the best, but I had an incredible view over the stadium, the LSU campus, and a sky brimming with stars. That night will always be a core memory for me, all thanks to ignoring those pesky doubts and just going for it.

As I looked up at the stars, tears came to my eyes as I realized I almost missed this opportunity. With each song, I felt increasingly confident that things are always working out for me. I experienced firsthand how true guidance should come from inner feelings, not from the mind.

Right then and there, I made a pinky promise to myself: listening to my intuition is top priority, now and forever. Above everything, I will trust and honor my intuition.

"I trust my intuition."

"My inner thoughts lead me to take the best path forward."

"I trust I am being guided in the right direction."

This is also an example of allowing our intuition to lead us to inspired action, which we will dive into in the next chapter.

Intuition, often described as a gut feeling or inner knowing, is a powerful and innate aspect of being human. It serves as our internal compass, providing guidance beyond the scope of logical reasoning. It's your gut feeling. I like to think it's a direct line to our higher being, one that knows what's best for our highest good. Understanding and trusting your intuition is the way to tap into a source of wisdom that transcends beyond the 3D reality we live.

You see, our bodies and minds just naturally run on intuition. It's an important tool in our toolbox. When you're breathing or your heart's beating—you don't even have to think about it. We're constantly engaging in natural movements, like turning our heads or walking, without consciously deciding to. It's our intuition that's silently directing and guiding each step, giving our brains the direction for each movement without us even realizing it.

When practicing affirmations, you've got to listen to that little voice inside. When you say your words and phrases, they should make you feel good, not uneasy or like something just ain't quite right. Tuning into your intuition is key to finding those affirmations that really speak to your heart.

One day I was taking my dogs for a long walk, and unexpectedly, the song *"Magic"* by Olivia Newton John randomly popped into my head. I started humming the tune, and then looked up the lyrics. Have you ever heard that song?

You have to believe we are magic
Nothin' can stand in our way
You have to believe we are magic
Don't let your aim ever stray
And if all your hopes survive, destiny will arrive

I'll bring all your dreams alive for you
I'll bring all your dreams alive for you

I believe this song references our inner being, our intuition, which will bring our dreams alive if we believe.

In the quiet whispers of intuition, we receive messages through gentle nudges guiding us towards this or that. It's like a soft voice amid the chaotic noise of your daily life. Learning to hear and understand these gentle, subtle signals is like discovering a secret language that guides you. Once you get the hang of tuning into your intuition, affirmations will start popping up in your mind out of nowhere. Take a moment to recognize these thoughts and say them out loud. Really listen to how you feel when you speak them—that's your inner guide talking.

The first house I found, I absolutely loved at first sight. But, you know, it didn't give me that rush of relief and excitement—it was just so pretty, and I rushed to put in an offer. Yet, something about it felt "off," and I couldn't quite see myself living there. I felt a bit anxious and unsettled. I tried to shrug it off because, well, buying a home is a huge deal and it's natural to second-guess a bit. But wouldn't you know it, the house failed inspection, and I wasn't one bit surprised. You see, I'd been affirming statements such as:

"I know I am attracting the perfect home for me."

"I trust that I will live in the perfect home."

"I am excited to find the house meant for me!"

Even saying those affirmations out loud, I could sense they just didn't fit with that particular house. My gut had already whispered to me that this wasn't my forever home.

We are all born with an innate messaging system. It's how we communicate our needs as infants. This system is a precious tool given to us at birth, so that we can communicate with the universe, our God, and our world. As we get older, we sometimes lose touch with our inner guidance system and tend to just go along with what everyone else wants or what seems expected of us by the world around us.

This habit of brushing aside our intuitive nudges and relying more on outside advice coming from others makes us doubt ourselves. This may look like searching for approval, value, and acceptance from our circle of friends and family, bosses, and coworkers, instead of trusting in our own inner strength. Forgetting how to trust our intuition can really throw us into a mess of anxiety and unease, and limits our beliefs.

Whenever we feel this kind of anxiety, it really takes looking inward to start trusting ourselves again, especially after big life changes like heartbreak, losing a job, dealing with grief, parenting challenges, and other pivotal moments.

Imagine facing a life changing decision, like whether to accept a new job, move across the country, or commit to a relationship or marriage. You may feel deep down that the situation is perfect for you and aligns with your long-term goals or personal values. However, we get bombarded with advice from friends and family urging us to do what they think, what's best for *them*.

Feeling pressured, you'll struggle with self-doubt and anxiety, torn between following your own intuition, which quietly suggests moving forward, and succumbing to the external validation and expectations of others. This inner conflict and the dissonance between your true desires and the external advice you receiving can lead to a state of anxiety, as you fear making a decision that could disappoint others or lead to regret if you don't listen to their own inner voice.

When we ignore our inner voice, we doubt our worth, regret our decisions, and forget how to set boundaries. In the end, we lose out either way. Using affirmations to keep you in a state of trusting yourself, acting on your intuition, and believing in yourself helps to fortify your sense of self-worth. It's like putting up a fence around your heart that only lets in what truly belongs. This way, you can make decisions that truly reflect who you are, not just what others expect of you. And goodness, when you live like that, you're not just surviving; you're thriving in your own beautiful, authentic way!

"I trust my inner guidance."

"I'm thriving!"

"I have clarity to make the right decisions by listening to my intuition."

"Things are always going my way."

The first few times you decide to trust your gut, you will feel a bit scared. Your body will react and might even resist you a little, like how I felt sick and panicked about the concert. That's your ego, the part of your decision-making that comes from the brain. The ego feels threatened when it's not in charge. The ego will get you to make decisions based on past trauma, PTSD, or your environment. Your mind urges you to follow the crowd. It warns, "Don't strike out on your own; people won't approve." But your intuition will never steer you wrong. You simply have to learn how to distinguish the two from each other. Affirmations can help in this process.

"My inner guidance gives me clarity."

"I am confident in my choices and trust my inner voice."

Focusing on our intuition and learning how it guides us prepares us for the true life that we want to build. Speaking out in faith puts the mind to rest and will keep a song of praise in your

41

heart. Control your thoughts, and you control your circumstances. One of my favorite songs to listen to is "Voice of Truth" by Casting Crowns. The lyrics flow with and resonate perfectly with this subject. Block out the negative and listen to who you really are. Forget the news, turn off the tv, stop scrolling on social media and instead, turn inward, and listen.

When coupled with affirmations, intuition can open a world that is bright and abundant, that feels easy and peaceful.

Your intuition, or gut feeling, comes right from the depth of your heart. Your heart does a lot more than just pump blood – it is remarkably similar to your brain, moving both blood and energy through the cells of your body. Some scientists have even begun to call it the "heart brain" because of the unique complex nervous system it possesses. So, when we talk about thinking from the heart, we're really just tuning into that intuition of ours.

Your heart knows just the right path to guide you on, and your brain holds all the know-how to help you take the steps and actions to get there. It's like the heart sets the destination, and the brain maps out the journey.

By paying attention to how certain things, ideas, and actions make you FEEL, you are tapping into your intuition and thereby activating your heart brain. Always check in with the heart, it will never steer you wrong. You just have to learn to listen to it.

42

Creating affirmations from the heart will feel good, peaceful, powerful. When you try empty affirmations, from the brain or ego, they will feel uncomfortable, or you will find it difficult to believe in them.

"I love figuring things out."

"I appreciate the unlimited options I have to choose from."

"I always make the right decisions because I know I'm being guided."

Now, there's a fine line when it comes to listening to your heart. This doesn't mean that if you are being treated unfairly or abusively by someone, you should ignore these actions just because you love them. Not at all. This is simply about honoring your true feelings and desires while also recognizing and respecting your own worth and boundaries. It's about making decisions that align with your well-being and personal growth, through intuition, rather than tolerating mistreatment in the name of love. Always remember that genuine love should uplift and support you, not bring you harm or distress.

When you're trying to understand your natural feelings about a subject, your body can help interpret these through emotions and sensations. It's like your body has a wisdom of its own, helping us understand what feels right or not-so-right.

Numerous books and videos explore the concept that your emotions can manifest as physical aches and pains in the body. I'd suggest diving into this subject if it feels intriguing to you.

I've learned to embrace that some days I just want to rest and do nothing. It's my body telling me to stop and take a breather. My intuition says "Rest, Relax, Rejuvenate." Other days I'm inspired to take on the world! Either way is fine, as long as you understand that your intuition is there giving you little nudges about what's best for you. When you listen, you keep picking up new ways to decode those subconscious clues.

Your body always knows what it needs. Millions of cells take their cues from your heart and brain, mixing in your energetic feelings to keep everything ticking right along. It's up to you to point it in the right direction. Speak affirmations to your cells:

"I am in good health and spirits."

"I feel happy and energetic today."

"Today, I am ready and able to get things done."

"Today, I have the clarity and confidence to attract success."

Energetic signals DO exist, and affirmations can be part of transformation and a healing process.

You see, if you're not up, you're down. If you're not above the line, you're below it. Nearly all thoughts originate from either a place of abundance or a place of scarcity. The key is to craft and express your affirmations from a mindset of abundance. When you are rich, you are not poor. When you are healthy, you are not sick. So, for instance, "I don't want to be sick anymore" contrasts with "I am healthy and strong." Which affirmation resonates more positively? Which thought aligns with your intuition? If you're accustomed to tuning into your intuition, you'll quickly shift the thought from one of lack to one of abundance. Practice framing your affirmations from various perspectives until you reach the point where they naturally reflect prosperity and optimism.

Energy plays a big part in intuition, too. We're always picking up on messages through the energy around us. Like when you walk into a room and immediately feel it's not your scene, or that prickly sensation when you sense someone is following you. Or think about those times you're thinking of someone and, wouldn't you know it, they call you right then. That's your intuition working through energy, sending you those quiet hints on what's going on. *"I am emitting positive energy to others"*—we'll unpack more about energy, or frequencies, later on in a chapter all its own.

In a world that constantly nudges us to meet others' expectations—be it as a polished professional at work, the perfect child, or an impeccable mother—we all deeply yearn to live true to our authentic selves, to be our best selves. This means we need to really listen to our intuition and our gut feelings to guide our decisions at every turn.

"I trust my intuition to guide me on the right path."

"My inner voice speaks clearly, and I listen with an open heart."

"My intuition is always right."

"I have the ability to hear the whispers of my intuition."

"I release fear and follow the guidance of my intuition."

"Each day, I strengthen my connection to my intuition."

"I trust my inner guidance system."

"I invite in my best life."

"I have the ability to figure things out."

"I invite in confidence and security to my life."

MY AFFIRMATIONS WORKSHEET

CHAPTER 3

‘‘

Living with Purpose and Intention

"You will also decree a thing, and it will be established for you; And light will shine on your ways."

Job 22:28

It's tempting to roll out of bed in the morning and simply go through the motions of waking up, getting dressed and run out the door on autopilot. How many times do we enter a room, attend a meeting, begin a new job, or even a new relationship with no preparation? What about our faulty expectations, or even no expectations at all? It's obvious that we, as humans on this busy and chaotic earth, are on autopilot more times than not. Most of the time, we think fearful thoughts, or no thoughts at all, about the actions we take throughout every minute of our day. Sort of like mindlessly drifting from experience to experience.

When you live and act with intention, you make sure you get the results you're after. To put it simply, the Bible tells us that

48

when you declare your intention, you pave the way for results, and the path ahead not only becomes clear, but it also lights up, guiding your next steps.

Without living intentionally, we end up setting faulty intentions without even realizing it. We judge situations without context, we fear outcomes, and our days unfold by chance rather than by design. But what if we took a moment to consciously set our intentions? We have the power to shape our days exactly how we want them. Why not make a deliberate effort to do just that?

Each morning as you wake up, do you think "I hate my job, this is going to be a terrible day"? If so, you are telling the universe, or setting the intention, that a terrible day is what you want to receive. You will notice you start to have awful experiences throughout the day because that is what you expect. That is what you asked for. That is what you will create.

I've been practicing setting intentions for a while now. Without setting my heart on having an awesome day and consciously deciding to live it out that way, I'd just be letting the world around me decide how my day's going to turn out. So here I am, watching the sun continue to rise, praying over my day, and claiming it's going to be a good one, because honey, I'm not about to let the hustle of life dictate my mood. No indeed.

Oh, what I would do to have blessings fall into my lap every day! What if we think that thought every morning? Did you know that we are capable of attracting and receiving everything we want and need? Setting intentions will start your day, meeting, event, conversation - whatever it is - with the power of blessings. You can command your day to be a peaceful one, filled with beautiful experiences, using your thoughts, affirmations, and intention. *"Today is a glorious day."*

Let me explain. We are what we think about. We get what we focus on. So, if you are focusing on the negative, you will get more negative. We're often taught to be cautious about what we ask for. People warn us not to ask for too much, we might come off as greedy or egotistical. But how can we receive our greatest blessings if we don't expect them? We often tuck away our grandest dreams, keeping them hidden deep in our hearts. Why does it seem wrong if we aim to hook the biggest fish in the pond using the power of our words? If we don't state clearly what we want, how will we receive it? Affirmations are ways to be sure we are focusing on attracting all things positive, along with our deepest desires.

When I owned my own sporting goods store, there were days I had no customers. The days when not a single person walked through my doors were hard to bear. My perfectly folded t-shirts, adorned with prints that I spent the most part of the day creating, were never seen. Some days it was heartbreaking. I'd stand by the wall of windows, watching the traffic pass me by and wonder what I was doing wrong. I was great at selling, even better at marketing, but I wasn't an expert at running a business. I knew this way down deep in my soul, yet I continued on.

My entire outlook shifted when I recognized how much I was learning through this business venture. I came to realize there were lessons hidden in the process of running the business, and in the newfound relationships I was cultivating. I made it my mission to learn something new every day—about my customers, my business, or my products. I set the intention *"Today, I am one step closer to where I'm meant to be."* With that intention and purpose in my step, I'd head into the store every day, and what do you know, the customers started coming in, too.

"Everyday in every way I am a success."

We spend too much of our time caught up in fear and doubt. Let me tell you, fear has a way of grabbing hold of your day and just delights in messing it all up. The anxiety and discord we may feel in the morning, or throughout the day, is always due to one thing - FEAR. Fear that we will encounter something unknown, something we will have to deal with, that will potentially ruin our day. Folks, I know you've heard this before, but FEAR IS A LIAR.

Fear is only our brain offering up protective thoughts submerged within our DNA from experiences we may not have even had during this lifetime. Most often, our fears and worries are about scenarios that are unlikely to occur. Fear is always due to our lack of knowledge about something – the future, the business, the relationship, our finances. It can paralyze the most confident and powerful among us if we let it have its way. Worrying is a surefire way to guarantee you will get exactly want you DON'T want. The antidote to fear, is to boldly proclaim positive words of victory over our lives. Set the intention *"I can handle this day with ease"*.

Wake up, think, and speak positive affirmations. Set the intention, or expectation, to have a fantastic day! *"I'm excited to see the great things that I attract today!"* Set the intention that your day will flow smoothly, the right people will appear to support you, the project will be completed, the traffic will be light, the day will bring new opportunities. *"I am grateful to wake up and be able to experience today."* Speak confidently of the day you want to have. Create the ideal scenario and speak it out loud. *"Thank you, God, for a day full of adventure!"* Get excited about the day first thing in the morning, and you will be surprised at how well your day turns out.

Most days I wake up and immediately look outside. I open all my blinds so the sunlight can come through. The soft grace of the sun shining helps me to slowly start my day with peace, and the chirping of birds fill me with thoughts of gratitude. I listen to their tweets and say, "Good Morning." I also holler a cheerful "Good Morning" to my dogs, just like the rooster announcing a new day. Their tails start wagging and they usually jump up and give me bunches of doggie kisses so how can I not smile and laugh and start each day on the right foot?

Intentionally establishing a morning routine sets the stage for a wonderful day and reminds us to live the day on purpose. I used to wake up feeling anxious and overwhelmed by the day's responsibilities, dwelling on yesterday's worries, or dreading upcoming meetings and outings. Sometimes, the thought of getting out of bed was daunting, and I had to coax myself to do simple things like having coffee or getting dressed. Luckily, I found a helper in Alexa, who plays my favorite upbeat music every morning at a specific time, spreading cheerful tunes throughout the house. I never truly understood the impact music has on my mood until it got me moving like a dance floor coming alive at a wedding reception! Even science agrees that music has healing properties. Thinking about this, I play music whenever I can. It helps me shape my outlook and tune out the rest of the world.

The best part about music is that most of the time, if you play the right songs, you'll get inspired to create new affirmations. Throughout the Bible, there are many references to hymns and songs of praise. If you sing along to the songs that make you feel good, you'll find all sorts of positive, motivating phrases. I've even created a playlist with the songs that correspond with my affirmations, and I play them every morning.

Living on purpose requires taking a step back from the hustle and bustle of being on autopilot. It is part of creating, instead of just dwelling. It is knowing with your entire being that things are always working out for you.

Every day is a new day! Better days are always ahead. Living with intention is keeping past problems in the past and understanding every negative situation is a chance to improve our resiliency and practice affirmations. Problems show us what we *don't* want, so we can work to create what we *do* want. We never know exactly when that ONE thing we have been waiting for will arrive. Act as if today is that day! Think peace. Think success. Think healing. Think growth.

"I am excited for this day!"

"I have everything I need to have a great day today!"

Once you get the hang of starting the day positive, upbeat, excited, and eager to face what's ahead, you'll notice somewhat of a hurdle. I don't know about you, but around 3 PM, just like clockwork—I hit that afternoon slump. It feels as though all my morning pep starts to fade, and I'm left dragging. My mind gets a little foggy, and my body feels like it's begging for a quick nap or a jolt of caffeine to get through the rest of the day. It's a real struggle to keep the momentum going!

Using intentional thought, I've rewired my brain to welcome this time, a cherished pause, a moment to stretch my legs, perhaps chat with a colleague, grab a coffee, and re-energize for the remainder of the day. Instead of complaining how tired I am, how I can't wait to leave work, or counting how many errands I have to run, I use this time to check in with myself and remind myself it's just a little time out. It's ok to take a break. We forget that it's unhealthy to always be busy, contrary to what we've been taught. Rest is a necessary part of life.

Find something that comforts you while reminding yourself, *"I feel ready to finish this day."* I sometimes play jazz music - Ella Fitzgerald, Sammy Davis, Jr., Johnny Mathis, Louis Armstrong – these artists calm my mind and put a smile on my face…setting my intention for the evening.

I'm telling you this because it sure did take me a while to figure out what works for me. Come afternoon, I'd hit that slump, and my energy would just plummet. Then, all those anxious thoughts and doubts would creep back in, making it a real struggle to keep my spirits up. I'd find myself praying for nightfall so I could just sleep those worries away. I coaxed myself out of this habit through morning intentional affirmations. *"I will maintain my energy and focus throughout the day."* This intention serves as a reminder when you hit that slump, helping you to recall and reconnect with your morning commitment.

Setting intentions is just a focused thought on what you want to experience. It is a deliberate act, a conscious decision, to guide your actions, thoughts, and emotions towards a particular direction. It helps you navigate through the day with purpose.

"I can do all this through him who gives me strength."
(Philippians 4:13)

Just as you would pray with intention, speak intentions through your affirmations. Know what your affirmations mean (remember they aren't empty words, wishes, or promises), and focus on the intent of the words. In other words, Mean What You Say, and Say What You Mean!

Stop spewing negative words! So many times, I catch myself thinking "I don't want to…" or "I'm struggling to…" Frame your intention in a positive light. Instead of focusing on what you want to avoid, express it in terms of what you plan to cultivate. For instance, "*I choose peace*" rather than "I want to avoid stress." Or "*I am ready to receive the solution to turn this around.*" Always repurpose negative into the positive. Remember, your words become reality. If you keep speaking about discouraging and dismal scenarios, that's exactly what you'll end up attracting.

Your intentions ought to be clear and realistic, and they should shine through in your affirmations. They should be specific and achievable. For example, my intentions have transformed from the more general "*I am going to have a good day*" into "*I see significant progress on completing my book.*"

Back when I worked as a Marketing Manager for an e-commerce company, we hired an intern to help us craft ads and content. We often found ourselves writing a lot of fluff—you know, those ads that throw around phrases similar to "We make life better" or "Elevate your life." Basically, what does that even mean? I got into the habit of asking my colleagues every day to read their sentences back and really think, "What specifically are you trying to convey?" It kind of became an office joke, but the question stands solid through to today. What are you trying to say to attract the result you want? Your affirmations can start out as generic, but be sure the intention is specific.

I look back now and laugh at some of the affirmations I used that were a bit too vague, and I could say they took my life in a different direction than I ever expected. When I was 8 months pregnant with my third child, we decided to move. The process of packing up an entire house while getting ready for a new baby was beyond exhausting. I remember saying out loud more than once, *"Next time I move, I'm buying all new stuff and won't have to pack a single box."* I hadn't set a real intention; I just spouted out an affirmation that set wheels in motion. It wasn't until I was forced to furnish a new home after Hurricane Katrina—where I'd lost absolutely everything, didn't pack a single box, and had to buy everything new, right down to Q-tips and cans of peas—that I remembered saying that statement four years earlier. Now, I'm a whole lot more specific with my affirmations!

Your intentions should also align with your values. Setting intentions throughout the day that reflect your identity and your beliefs ensures that it remains a practical and motivating force in your daily tasks.

"Today, I offer kindness and understanding to everyone I meet."

"I am courageous and strong."

"I love honoring my commitments with others."

"I am capable of practicing forgiveness."

As mentioned, external forces will kick in as that ego realizes it's no longer in control. Each time you practice an intentional affirmation, it's like throwing a punch in a battle against doubt. When fear arises, speak to it. Don't let it fester. Face it. If you give it time to grow, it will infiltrate your cells, overwhelm your mind, and cripple your ability to create. Instead, speak out loud "*I shall not fear*". I sometimes say, "*Go away fear, you are a liar*" followed by "*I am strong and capable*," or "*I am safe*." In this case, reminding yourself that there is no place for fear and doubt to live amidst your thoughts.

Whenever something gets under my skin, I tend to say, *"I'll figure it out."* Now, some folks (like my Mom) might get a tad annoyed when I pull that line, but it just gives me a moment to mull things over and listen to my intuition to find the right answer. It's my little way of giving myself some breathing room to sort things out properly. It's a mental pause to give my intuition the chance to catch up to my circumstances. I can break the problem down and really set my mind on what I want to see happen. It's like laying out my intentions plain and clear, so I know exactly where I'm headed.

Your intentions may shift daily as your experiences evolve. Let's say one of your core values is authenticity. In this case, your intention might be to express your true self more openly in your personal and professional life. You might make a conscious effort to express your thoughts and feelings more often. Your career intention might involve seeking a job or joining projects or clubs that allow you to be true to yourself and your values. You might choose activities and relationships that resonate with your true self, and respectfully decline those that do not. You would also align your affirmations with these values. For instance, the affirmations could be:

"I love that I work with others of the same mindset and values."

"I am unique and capable of expressing my true self."

"I invite supportive and compassionate people into my life."

I once met some like-minded girlfriends at a conference. Before I even boarded the plane, I set the intention to do something spontaneous and fun, outside my comfort zone. I love thinking outside the box, but when it comes to acting outside of it, my brain usually talks me right back into the boring box.

After a late dinner, while walking back to the hotel, we passed by the pool. The water shimmered under the moonlight, the fountains still flowing, and the sound of rushing water made us all glance at each other with the same thought—should we jump in? At first, I held myself back. My brain kicked into high gear...

"My clothes will get wet, There are no towels, I should really go to bed, We have an early start tomorrow." But then, someone yelled, "I'm going in!" and before my boring brain could stop me, I remembered my intention: *"I am spontaneous and do things that make me laugh!"* Without a second thought, I dove right into the deep end, fully clothed in business attire. No regrets!

Remember, setting intentions sets you up for success. When you set your intention, it puts you in charge and opportunities will appear all around you. Be as specific as possible. Living with intention means that each task is done on purpose. Each task leads you to the outcome you expect. So, start small. If your goal is to go to an exotic island for vacation, your intentions and affirmations my look something like *"I love experiencing new cultures"* and or *"Today I will learn one thing about traveling overseas"* and then google exotic islands to give yourself that knowledge to set up the path forward.

The bible contains scriptures that highlight the value of purposeful thinking and deliberate action.

"Commit your work to the LORD, and your plans will be established." (Proverbs 16:3)

In other words, speak your intention, through prayer and affirmations, and the steps forward, and inspired action, are shown to you through intuition.

By pairing affirmations with concrete actions aligned with your intention, you create a powerful synergy aligned with your goal. This is how you design your life. Open a new savings account (for when you get a raise), Clean out your closet (to make space for your new partner when he moves in), Rearrange your mugs so that your favorites are front and center (to prepare each day with a smile). And trust your wants will be delivered.

Close your eyes and envision the positive impact of your intention and affirmation working for you. Visualizing success reinforces your commitment to your intentions, and can boost positive thinking. Setting an intention isn't merely a one time act or thought. It has a ripple effect on your mindset, actions, and interactions with others. As you embody your intention, you contribute positively to your immediate surroundings, fostering what is called an "intentional existence." Meaning that you are living your life on purpose, and building it the way you intend it to be.

The world gets brighter, and life gets sweeter with every new day you live on purpose.

♥

"I am choosing the right thoughts to create a better reality."

"I am designing my own life."

"I live and breathe my authentic self in everything I do."

"I am open to limitless opportunities the universe serves me."

"Things are always working out for me."

"Today is a good day."

"I am attracting clarity and focus for my daily tasks."

"I am grateful for this peaceful day."

"I allow myself to attract good things into my life."

"I know I am on the right path."

"Everyday in every way I attract wonderful experiences."

MY AFFIRMATIONS WORKSHEET

CHAPTER 4

Staying Above the Line

"Do not conform to the pattern of this world, but be transformed by the renewing of your mind."

Romans 12:2

In previous chapters, I hinted at a metaphor that described the feeling of being in the state of emitting positive energy. I used the term "stay above the line." But, what exactly is the "line"? This figurative line is an invisible boundary that divides positive energy from negative, where anxiety and despair reside far beneath excitement and abundance. You've heard similar phrases reflecting this idea such as "Rise up!" or "Forgive and forget" or "Be the better person." It's essentially the same concept.

At a young age in elementary school, we learned about atoms, ions, protons, and such, and recognized energy as the foundation of our world. We were introduced to the different types of energy, but our teachers didn't really go much deeper than a general lesson. We surely weren't taught how to harness this energy to our own benefit.

As we go about our lives, interacting and sharing experiences with one another, like when we meet at church, at work, or just at the grocery store—we are shaped into who we are by how we connect with each other. We begin to understand how we can feel energy, and how energy can make us feel. We even learn that there are people who can actually see energy. We talk about the "energy in the room" and "good vibes." We begin to know that energy is everywhere, but what exactly is it doing? How is it affecting our lives?

When we align our energy to the right state of being, and attune to the right frequency of the universe, magic happens.

If you're in a terrible mood, stewing in angry or confused thoughts, and you start rattling off affirmations, you might as well be talking to the wind. You've got to calm your heart first before those affirmations can take root, or you're wasting your time. It's like saying yes, when you want to say no, while shaking your head "no". It won't work. You can't trick the universe. You can't trick your maker. He knows the true you. Affirmations are not magic. You must be in the right state of mind for them to work. You need to be above that line to match your inner energy with your desires.

Positive words are just the thing to gently and deliberately guide you into a better state of mind.

"I don't have to figure this out now."

"This too shall pass."

"Things always work out for me."

"I am safe."

These affirmations will help you to move to a lighter energy, (above the line), and help change your perspective. Sometimes, even with those lingering negative feelings, affirmations can help you make it through the day. Often, after I've tucked myself in bed, and even if I feel like my affirmations didn't do any good, I find myself waking up the next day feeling a whole lot better.

Friends, if you're muttering "I hate my job" one minute and then demanding, "Ok universe, you better give me a better job" the next, do you really think that's going to work? The answer is a loud and clear NO. Affirmations only work when you're truly ready to accept your blessings. They're not about issuing ultimatums or stewing in anger. It's about opening your mind and your heart and having faith that everything will work out. It's about shaping the life you want by actively molding your experiences and choices.

When working with affirmations amidst a struggle or challenge, it is important to take some time and ground yourself, or relax and clear your mind, before you begin. Be present with the moment, take a deep breath, and empty your mind of thoughts. It only takes a second or so to do this. This pause is especially important to set the intention of the affirmation.

When I set out to write this book, I had the perfect title in mind. I was all fired up to weave together the words and chapters under that banner. But then I learned I couldn't use the title for various reasons, and let me tell you, I was just about heartbroken. It felt like all my plans just flew right out the window. I threw myself a two-minute pity party, but then it hit me—this was just the universe nudging me to compose something even better. As I calmed down and realigned myself, I realized that if I wasn't tuned in just right to the higher frequency, the perfect title wouldn't pop into my head. As soon as I started to really think it through, and worked through my affirmations, a new concept dawned on me, and I was more thrilled than ever before.

"I trust in the universe to guide my creativity, knowing that every challenge leads me to greater opportunities."

"Thank you, God, for protecting me and leading me to something better."

"Solutions are always being revealed to me."

Remember, affirmations aren't just words. You have to FEEL them. Believe in them. Only then will you rise to the proper frequency to receive all their benefits.

When I talk about the word 'frequency' it might sound rather confusing. I'll admit, it has taken me years to grasp even a portion of what this means in terms of manifestation and how to use it. It isn't just being in a positive state of mind. **It is rising up, with every fiber of your being, to the most positive, whole, feeling of completeness.** It is experiencing a feeling of such pure joy and satisfaction that you get chills going up and down your entire body. It is expanding into the energy of joy, anticipation, and excitement. Even for a moment, achieving a higher frequency, a good vibration, can be physically felt and will attract huge benefits with positive effects on your life. Only then will you meet your hopes and dreams where they are.

A good friend always reminds me to "Get Excited!" whenever I'm about to go through a major change. The fear of change can be powerful, and it's easy to mistake excitement for fear. But when you start to get excited about the opportunities around you, and genuinely appreciate the present, that excitement *can* and *will* replace fear.

The feeling of excitement has the power to completely transform the tone of any situation. For example, imagine you're about to give a big presentation. Initially, you might feel nervous and overwhelmed by negative thoughts. However, if you shift your perspective to see the presentation as an exciting opportunity to share your knowledge and ideas, that excitement can instantly turn those negative thoughts into positive ones. *"This is going to be so much fun."* This shift not only boosts your confidence but also energizes you, making it easier to engage and connect with your audience.

This is the exact advice we need to bump up from a medium vibration to a high flying feeling of excitement and joy. With zero fear, we increase frequency to meet all the good things where they are. *"I am excited to see opportunities unfold before me."*

Always be open to and ready for miracles to find you.

Affirmations will never work in a place of negativity or lack. You MUST work on your frame of mind, your vibration, your perspective.

Even in the Bible, it says **"Finally, brothers and sisters, whatever is true, whatever is noble, whatever is right, whatever is pure, whatever is lovely, whatever is admirable-if anything is excellent or praiseworthy-think about such things." (Philippians 4:8)** In other words, always focus on the good.

We all face circumstances where it feels there is no way out. It gets hard to see the good in any of it. Our minds have a way of slipping into negative thinking out of habit. But, finding the good really only takes a few seconds if we pause and look for it. Affirmations can help, but you must recognize the good in your life to combat the negative frequency.

When I had to deal with a toxic boss, I'd often see them as a full-on bully, charging at me like a wild animal. Something had to change, and it was clear it wouldn't be their attitude. I changed my perspective and started seeing this bully boss as an immature individual, insecure in their position of authority, using every insult they shot at me as a win for them. My affirmations sounded something like:

"My focus is on my success, and I am successful."

"I am proud of my work ethic, and I am capable of completing my tasks."

"I know the perfect job is on its way to me."

I turned my attention to finding a new job and got excited about new possibilities. I stopped paying attention to this boss and ignored their bullying. Eventually, when that boss would come at me with their insults and harassment, I'd just smile. They didn't rattle me anymore, because I knew this wasn't my forever job. It was like watching a storm blow in—I stayed steady, knowing it

71

would pass. I did everything I could to stay above the line, and sure enough, that miserable person eventually blew right on out of my life.

I rose to a higher frequency that no longer matched theirs.

I raised my vibration to attract a job and the type of boss that was right for me.

Everyone emits a frequency, or what you call a vibration. It's reflected in our discernment of good vibes and bad vibes. Each person, place, and thing emits a frequency that we can feel and sense. This is why your vibe attracts your tribe! We are like magnets, attracting things to us at all times. Staying in a high vibration (good energy) attracts other highly vibrating things (and people), to you. Good vibrations attract good vibrations.

Your goal should be to vibrate so high that toxic people and situations fall away from you because they no longer know how to survive in your energy.

In my mind, I visualize frequency like steps in a stadium, with each row containing all the experiences and things we attract. It doesn't matter the size of the desire or how complex you think it may be in order to reach it. Everything lives on a frequency and it's our job to match the frequency of the things we desire.

We need to meet our blessings at their level, which means raising our thoughts, actions, and energy to align with what we truly want. It's about tuning in to that higher frequency, focusing on what excites and motivates us, and letting go of the doubts or negativity that hold us back. Only by stepping into that mindset can we attract the opportunities and outcomes we're aiming for.

This ability to tune in to different frequencies is another tool we've been given to connect with everything in the universe.

Now before you try to change your frequency to simply get *things*, it works a bit differently than that. Think of how the things you want will make you *feel*, and then align with that feeling. In my experience, the frequency of blessings lives in the feeling of having them. It is why we are always told count our blessings even during the times it's most difficult to do so.

The frequency of abundance is on the same stadium row as the *feeling* of being abundant. Easier said would be if you want a million dollars, think of what having a million dollars would FEEL like. Would it give you the feeling of freedom, safety, happiness, joy, vibrant, confidence? That feeling is what you are aiming for, not the actual thing. Ever hear someone say "I feel like a million bucks"...that's the goal! When you feel that good, when you radiate that kind of positive energy, you naturally attract things that resonate with those good vibes.

Music has a wonderful way of shifting both your own energy and the atmosphere around you. Put on some upbeat tunes or whatever kind of music lifts your spirits—I'm partial to some upbeat Christian songs myself. And of course, don't underestimate the power of moving your body! Whether it's dancing, walking, or just stretching, it shakes up any stagnant energy inside you and truly breathes new life into your day, both literally and figuratively. Just think about how refreshed and invigorated you feel after a good long walk or a quick dance around the kitchen. That burst of positivity? That's you hitting the high frequency of good energy.

Think of it like this, using the stadium idea: all the good stuff—love, joy, your dream job, your soulmate, perfect health, clear thinking, even that favorite dessert from the best spot in town—is up there in the top rows of the stadium. Now, on the other hand, the not-so-great things like struggling to make ends meet, flat tires, missed opportunities, or health troubles, well, those are down on the bottom rows. And right there in the middle? That's where you'll find the line, and things that don't really stir you one way or the other, like little answers to everyday problems or small steps that are part of the journey to your dreams.

As you begin to understand energy and frequency, you take an invisible step to the next highest row. You climb metaphorically from the bottom row up and into the highest energy level, the highest frequency, aligning with the things you desire. Picture a gate to the VIP section opening and you walk right through it.

Stacks of blessings are there. It's as if you arrived at the warehouse where all your desires were just delivered, ready for you to claim.

Once you rise to the top of the stadium steps, everything you desire is now within your reach. You are now above the line. Notice all the doors that open for you when you are in a high vibration. And notice the opposite…when you are angry, hasty, negative, you end up with a flat tire on the side of the road. Because that experience lives in the lower part of the stadium, the lower frequency. You have the choice to surround yourself with the things and experiences on either the bottom level or the VIP level.

Affirmations are a mighty tool to clear your mind and tweak your frequency, but they're not a cure-all. They won't instantly catapult you from gloom to glee, but they sure can help you shift your perspective and assist in turning things around. Affirmations can halt that downward spiral into darkness and despair, giving you a moment's relief to start climbing toward a better mood. For example, if you can move from anger to just being irritated, that's progress! And inching up from eagerness to passion? That's one step closer to pure joy.

Keep in mind, it's all about the feeling—that's what we're aiming for. You'll find all sorts of charts and graphs online that lay out the spectrum of feelings, from the lowest to the highest. Our task is to always reach for the feeling that's just a notch above the one we're currently experiencing. Doing this shifts our frequency upwards.

Once you get into the habit of positive affirming each morning to set up a positive high frequency day, everything will come to you as if you are a magnet, attracting all that you have dreamed of. Reciting affirmations throughout the day keeps you focused on the good. This is how you design the life you want.

Keeping your high frequency centers on not letting anything shake your mood. It's all about how you feel in the moment. Immediately when you wake up in the morning, speak your affirmations and you will feel how your intentions are set for the day. It is easy to wake up and fall back into the drama and problems of the past day. But every day is a new day. Wake up as if it's the first day of your life, and you have new opportunities and new experiences to discover. Set your intention and commit to staying open and hopeful for a perfect day. Don't allow others to drag you down with their drama, problems, and despair. You can be a good friend and listen, but always keep in the back of your mind *"Things always work out for me."* Speak as if this day is going to be just exactly as you want it to be. Ask yourself *"What if today is the best day of my life?"*

As you state affirmations, whether morning or night, you can feel your body come alive to the positive moving energy in and all around you. Pay attention to how your body feels. I usually feel energy moving as if I can feel my blood coursing through my veins. I feel a little bit of electricity as if something really good is about to happen. I feel excitement, joy, love. I listen to my heartbeat, and it feels fuller and more powerful than ever before. I visualize myself laughing and loving and just floating above everything that is on this earth. This is the moment you want to never let go of. You want to keep this momentum going as long as you can, as if you are a superpower, able to do anything you set your mind to and even beyond that.

This is the level of energy you strive to maintain all day long. I'm not going to lie to you, it is very difficult to maintain this feeling and this frequency for more than a few minutes because your daily life events will pull you down. You deal with the business of the day, low energy people, mundane tasks, traffic jams, etc. But this is the work that we have to do. The work is to make a choice at each second, each moment, to stay in the highest frequency that you can. I remind myself during the day many times to stay above the line.

Visualize the line that separates each frequency. The "stay above the line" method that I use simply reminds myself at each moment to ignore the petty things that drag me down. I say to myself *"stay above the line"* whenever I start to worry, doubt, have anxiety, see something negative, hear something negative, or get frustrated. Learning to recognize a shift in your perspective takes a lot of time and practice. And pulling myself back up, or keeping myself on a high frequency, is extremely hard. Just acknowledging that I am falling below the line causes a drop in frequency, it's that quick. But just like tuning to a specific radio channel, you won't find what you're looking for if the dial is on the wrong frequency. Have you ever accidentally hit the AM/FM tuner button on your radio, and it took you at least a minute to figure out how to get it back to the FM station? Just like that, it happens quickly, accidentally, and takes a minute to sort out what happened. Be patient, allow yourself a moment, and then choose to move towards tuning into the frequency you desire.

"I have everything I need."

"I am blessed."

"I can do this."

Once you start practicing this, you will begin to notice subtle changes and "coincidences" that show up for you. Things just seem to start working out. You may label this as a coincidence but trust me it is not. This is the law of attraction working for you through aligning your frequency and energy with your deepest desires. All of a sudden, you're at the top stadium seats, in the VIP section, and everything you want or need is at your fingertips.

I experience this <u>all the time</u>! One example is when I needed to find the perfect dress for my daughter's wedding. After slipping into two or three formal gowns, I just lost the desire to continue. I was beginning to dread the process and my thoughts kept circling to "I'm never going to find one," or "I'm just going to settle with the first one that fits well." After a couple of weeks of this feeling, I woke up one Saturday morning and decided to change my perspective. I spent some time speaking affirmations and setting my intention for the day.

"Today is the day I'm going to find the perfect dress."

"The perfect dress is just waiting for me."

"I can't wait to look absolutely gorgeous in the perfect dress."

Guess what happened? I found the perfect dress! I actually found a few of them, but one in particular felt it was made just for me!

Boy, was I on the right frequency.

Later that day, I had a random thought about Girl Scout cookies. I spotted the Scouts in front of a store while driving by and realized it was that time of year again. I got to thinking all about the flavors I like, how good they tasted, just sort of dreaming about the cookies while picturing them (the caramel coconut ones are my faves!). I wasn't thinking about these cookies on purpose, it was just a natural thought that popped in my head. As soon as I moved on to a different thought, I was interrupted by my doorbell ringing and wouldn't you know, it was the girls selling cookies. I said to myself when I answered the door "of course it is you."

I started recognizing that when I was on the right frequency, things that I would think of no matter how small or large, would appear before me. If I was waiting for a phone call, the moment I adjusted my frequency to "above the line", the phone would ring. Or an answer I've been searching for would pop in my head. Or a fantastic idea would take form. Strangers would seek me out among a crowd just to talk with me, sometimes saying just the things I needed to hear at that moment. Solutions and opportunities would fall into my lap, and choices would become crystal clear, as if I opened up a book with all the answers.

It is up to us to harness this feeling, this frequency, and stretch it out as long as we can.

Once, I was on a long drive during a bright, sunny day. The sun was shining through the clouds, directly into my eyes. My sunglasses just weren't strong enough to block the rays and I was playing around with my car visor to keep a good view of the road. I thought "maybe I should splurge on a good pair of sunglasses?" I've never spent any decent money on a nice pair, mostly because I tend to lose them. But this time, I felt like I should consider shopping for some when I got back home. I thought about buying some Ray-Bans. As I pictured the style I'd like to buy, a catchy song came on the radio, and I forgot about it as quickly as it had crossed my mind.

Two days later, my son approached me and the first sentence out of his mouth was, "Here mom, here's your sunglasses." He had his hand held out with a bright shiny new pair of Ray Ban sunglasses, the same style I was imagining to own. Immediately I said, "Oh my gosh, where did you get these?" He shrugged his shoulders and replied that he didn't know. He explained how he had found them in his car and figured they were mine. I remembered I had used his car the previous day for about a quick errand, and definitely didn't see any sunglasses lingering around. I repeated to him that they weren't mine and he replied with "Well, they are yours now."

The universe works in mysterious ways, but it is all designed by you. There is a special law of cause and effect which is accepted by scientists and people all over the world. But this law of attraction exists right alongside of it, and it is based on frequency. While you practice learning how it feels to move between frequencies, you reap the benefits of this law.

When doubt starts to creep in, stop it immediately with an affirmation, spoken out loud. Change the negative to a positive.

Instead of saying "I'm so scared of what the results are going to be" say *"I trust that everything is working out for me"* or *"I know that my body is capable of healing."*

One of my favorite speeches I give myself whenever doubt starts creeping in or I'm faced with a tough decision or situation is that I don't have to decide this now. *"I don't have to figure this out now"* and give yourself time to rise to the frequency of solutions and blessings.

The moment you begin to notice the impact of putting your tools and God-given resources to work, you begin to create a joyous life.

"I love and appreciate this moment and am excited about what is unfolding."

"I see blessings in every part of my life."

"I know I attract solutions with ease and grace."

"My life is full of joy and peace."

As your frequency improves, your world shifts along with it.

♥

"I have everything I need, and the universe supports me."

"I attract positive energy everywhere I go."

"I am safe and protected."

"The right people always show up at the right time."

"I am excited for all of the opportunities around me."

"I am open and receptive to all good things."

"I see opportunities clearly and often."

"I am confident & good thoughts fill every cell of my being."

"I trust the journey of my life."

"Everything I desire is on its way to me."

"I have unlimited potential."

"I am worthy of accomplishing my goals & living my perfect dream life."

"I can have whatever I want."

"I am open and ready to receive all of my amazing blessings."

MY AFFIRMATIONS WORKSHEET

CHAPTER 5

Take Inspired Action

"Be still before the Lord and wait patiently for him; do not fret when people succeed in their ways, when they carry out their wicked schemes."

Psalm 37:7

As humans evolve, we realize more and more that we were created to endure the ebb and flow of life. People and things will move in and out of our lives, and we are meant to shift with ease from one thing to another. We aren't designed for the relentless grind and intense hustle of the rat race. Sure, we can achieve worldly and lofty goals by going against the grain, sometimes trying to succeed 1,000 different ways until the one way clicks into place.

But what if there was an easier way? What if by simply pausing and listening to your intuition, you'd receive the answer to your question? What if aligning to the right energy level, and speaking affirmations would bring clarity to your choices and decisions? What if feeling excited and staying above the line gave you ideas that made life's work much easier and more pleasant?

Welcome to inspired action.

One of the best byproducts of affirmations and meditations is inspired action. Have you ever had a thought just pop into your head that felt like a nudge to take action? Have you been on a walk and felt the need to call a friend? Have you been sitting in silence and had an idea to write a book or paint a picture? This is called inspired action. Inspired actions are steps that are guided by a sense of inspiration, inner guidance, or intuition. It's the desire God places in your heart, and when you follow it, things seem to fall into place.

Best of all, when it's inspired action, your confidence and boldness is at a level you cannot achieve by simple human means. The action resonates so intensely with your core, that you absolutely cannot NOT do it. You feel it in your entire being, you know it's right, and the path ahead begins to light up.

You can use affirmations to increase inspired action the same way you pray for God to show you the way.

"I am living my dream life."

"I have everything I need to move forward in my path."

"I am where I am supposed to be right now."

"I see clearly my future steps and trust they lead me to my destiny."

"I am ready to receive."

"I invite success into my life."

Taking inspired action toward your goals is a crucial component of manifestation. You win when you learn how to align your actions with your affirmations to bring about your most desired outcomes.

Everything that unfolds in your future is shaped by the actions you take today.

Before I had my own business, I'd stand right in the middle of my living room and declare my affirmations out loud. One of them was a firm belief that I would find a job where I could make a real difference and learn more about running a business. Back then, I was just picking myself up after losing everything to Hurricane Katrina, feeling quite low but still holding on to hope that I would be okay.

One morning, I felt an unmistakable tug, a super strong message—it was as if something was urging me, almost forcing me, to check the job listings. I remember this moment distinctly. At that moment, my TV was playing an episode of the old 70's sitcom "Three's Company". I wasn't really paying attention, sort of mindlessly watching the screen. In a quick moment, a signal or lightbulb went off, like a quick burst of insight. I instantly fired up my computer, went straight to the job board, and there it was: the perfect job for me. I applied, and sure enough, I was hired. This role launched me into a new chapter of my career, and every job afterward hinged on the experience I gained from it. Inspired action led me to take that specific action that designed my entire future.

I tend to believe that if I had ignored that feeling and not acted on its message, I may have struggled in my career, ended up in jobs I didn't enjoy, or forced success in ways that didn't feel natural. I'd much rather be inspired to act, rather than struggle.

Another way to explain inspired action is as if someone is standing over your shoulder, telling you how to move forward but that someone is you - your intuition.

The Scriptures tell us more than once to **"Be Still."** When we quiet down our minds and emotions—not all caught up in anger, anxiety, or grief—we can really tune into our intuition. That's when we can hear the messages meant just for us. These messages encourage us to take inspired action, rather than forcing things to occur. And, when you move with that kind of guidance, you'll find things start falling into place a whole lot easier.

Once, when I was looking for an unusual adventure, I signed up for a silent retreat. Now, as I've mentioned in this book—and if you know me at all—you can imagine that was no small feat. Keeping quiet for three whole days? Friends were placing bets on whether I'd last or call it quits early.

While I was there, I'd sit in silence by a pond each evening, surrounded by the usual suspects—lizards, bees, ducks, birds, spiders, ants, and wasps. One evening, a huge wasp came along, and I was sure I was going to get stung. But I remained as still as a statue, even when it landed just an inch away from my arm. I watched it, not moving a muscle, and after a few seconds, it flew off.

I thought to myself, "What a good analogy for being still despite your circumstances!" I jotted down this story, thinking one day I'd share it with y'all. It turned out to be the heart of the onset of this book, all sparked by that one still moment, and my decision to follow through on a bit of inspired action.

Inspired action can also be found during moments of daily activity. I speak about career often as examples, but it's a subject that we can all understand easily. Let's say you desperately want to be promoted to management but are always passed up for promotions. You may feel frustrated and your self-worth starts to decline. You wonder if you should take action - quit your job or change your career. Trying affirmations like *"I am worthy of a promotion,"* and *"I am capable of managing others,"* and *"I am skilled to manage others successfully"* will help, but sometimes that still leaves you with self-doubt surrounding the situation.

When you pause, let go of any negative emotions about your situation, and just listen to your intuition, you might find yourself struck by a new, actionable idea. Does it nudge you towards taking some management classes, or joining a group of entrepreneurs? Maybe it's prompting you to call a friend or pick up a book? It may cause you to see things in a different perspective, or a new affirmation forms in your mind that feels really good to speak. It only takes <u>one</u> conversation, <u>one</u> chance meeting, <u>one</u> result of an inspired action to change your life forever.

Most of the time, inspired action comes in small steps, tiny thoughts. It might be something as simple as deciding to take the day off and bumping into an old friend. Or it might guide you to exactly where you need to be, like when you choose to cook burgers for dinner and then notice you left the milk out on the counter as you head into the kitchen. It can be solutions that come when you are confused about what to do next, and when you take action, the rest of the path forward begins to light up one step at a time.

Have you ever heard the saying, "When you lose something, it shows up when you least expect it?" That's because your intuition already knows where the lost item is and gives you little nudges to take inspired action toward finding it.

When I decided to write this book, I felt inspired to write it. I was driven by thought it would help someone, even if it was only one person. I had no idea where to start. After reminding myself *"I can create my life"* and *"I have the capacity to share my blessings with others,"* I was moved to take the actions that led to my attendance at the retreat that I mentioned at the beginning of this book.

I typically watch inspirational YouTube videos, but this particular day I was hopeful to find something new, and kept scrolling and scrolling and scrolling. I was inspired to randomly click on an unusual video that normally I would just pass by. I let my intuition lead me and I sat and watched the entire video (which was about relationships and love). At the end of the video, there was a quick 10 second plug about an upcoming retreat. That little voice inside me told me I should explore this idea (inspired action).

That retreat was a major life changer for me. I can't imagine the decisions I would be making or the life I would be living had I not attended this retreat. It was a full blown, life changing five days that offered the type of transformative energy that I had never felt before. I left with such confidence and an improved sense of worth, strength, and empowerment.

After the retreat, I felt compelled to start journaling every day, writing down my ideas, experiences, anything that meant something to me, no matter how big or small. Once the writing began, I was able to organize my thoughts, and a path of authoring a book on my own became clear.

I didn't jump on it right away, being the overthinker I am. After all, who doesn't approach a big project with a bit of fear and insecurity?

But suddenly, out of nowhere random people started showing up in my life that had written and published their own books. I would meet up with friends and they would spontaneously say to me, "Wow, you should write a book." Everywhere I turned, there was mention of books being written and authors to meet. I literally can't make this up. Every actionable step that I took based on my intuition, one by one, led me to the decision to author this book. The popular saying you only have to take the first step is true. The key is to allow it to come from inspiration.

When you make a conscious effort to align your actions with your affirmations, you propel yourself forward on your desired path. Allow your heart to guide you into realizing the difference between inspired and forced action. While affirmations create positive mental images, thoughts, and feelings - taking inspired action transforms that positivity into progress and helps you move forward. Forced action will feel uncomfortable, unrewarding, and exhausting. Practice noticing when deliberate steps move you closer to the feeling of happiness and success, then celebrate these small steps. Show gratitude with your affirmations after each good-feeling action. Doors will continue to open. Things will magically show up for you.

I'm constantly reminded that inspired action is a true blessing. Story after story of things falling into place just right reinforces that acting on inspired action is the best way to live.

Once, I was interviewing for a consulting job and needed to prove I held a high-ranking position at a company that had closed its doors. All I had to show for it was a business card with my title printed on it that was nowhere to be found. I scoured the house for it, but as the clock ticked down to my next therapy appointment, I had to let it go.

During the therapy session, we dove into a discussion about "authenticity" and what it means to not just speak your mind but to be yourself more fully. It was a topic that piqued my interest, and I had a heap of questions we barely got to scratch the surface of.

When I got back home, I flipped on the TV and surprise, surprise! There on the screen was a show featuring an author discussing none other than the topic of authenticity. Talk about a coincidence! (wink, wink!) That jogged my memory—I remembered I actually own that author's book. I dashed to my bookshelf, hoping to dig a little deeper into our therapy topic. And guess what? When I opened the book, right there on the very page I needed to read, was the single, lost business card I'd been searching for all along, acting as a bookmark.

What a fantastic example of action inspired by my intuition, along with results from my affirmations.

You can't make this stuff up!

Picture inspired action like the universe handing you the spark to light your flame. You're one of a kind, with a purpose unlike anyone else on this earth. Uncovering and living out that purpose takes time—it's about letting it reveal itself in ways that truly light up your path. When you design your life, you're not just making choices; you're shaping the life you're drawn to, the life you're meant to live. It's all about crafting that deep-down, soul-satisfying life you know you're supposed to have.

Sometimes, we don't take action because we think that our dreams are just too big. "I'll never be a millionaire," "I'll never have what that person has"—those kinds of doubts sneak in because we can't yet see the steps to get there. We get hung up on the "how." But here's the secret: you gotta let go of worrying about how it's all going to come together. Affirmations aren't there to give you a step-by-step guide; they're there to spark your spirit and help you carve out your own special path. We can't always see how things will unfold, but we must believe and truly KNOW that they will. Sometimes, just taking that first step is enough to inspire us to jump further or just move on to the next little step. Each step is like the ship moving us forward to our goals and intentions, affirmations are the river in which the ship is flowing.

Sometimes, inspired action is to do nothing.

Maybe the timing just isn't right, or things aren't quite lined up. Maybe you're not yet strong enough for what you're asking for. Think about it—when you pray for patience, life suddenly throws you situations where you gotta practice just that. If you rush in and try to force something before you're ready, you're setting yourself up for a tough ride. Do you plant seeds and then stand over them hollering, "Grow! Grow! Grow!"? Of course not. We trust that the good Lord and the universe will provide what those seeds need to thrive—the rain, the soil, the critters, all of it. So why is it so hard to have that same faith in ourselves?

Your intuition will always give you the answers. But you have to practice being attuned to its messages. Your frequency, your energy, your words, thoughts, all of which will help you hear the messages from your deepest self. Follow the energy. Follow your feelings. Be okay with waiting. Practice patience and faith that all is working out for you in divine timing. Align your affirmations with your intuition and take action when inspiration strikes.

♥

"I am ready to take inspired action towards my goals."

"Every step I take is guided by a powerful purpose."

"I trust my instincts and take bold action towards my dreams."

"I am a creator of my destiny, taking inspired steps each day."

"I am fueled by passion & take action with determination."

"I am confident in myself to always make the right decisions."

"My actions align with my goals, creating my path to success."

"I am strong in my ability to take action towards my dreams."

"Each action I take brings me closer to all that I desire."

"I am in tune with the rhythm of inspiration & act upon it decisively."

MY AFFIRMATIONS WORKSHEET

CHAPTER 6

Visualizing Victory

"Commit to the Lord whatever you do, and he will establish your plans."

Proverbs 16:3

Before our dreams come to pass, we've got to let them sink into our hearts and minds. The scriptures tell us to write the vision, speak it into existence, and meditate on it. When we imagine our most precious outcomes, we must also have faith they will come to pass. Visualization is a key step to embracing an affirmation practice. It is the process that helps you see your desires as if they are already real, expands the feelings associated with achieving them, and closes the gap between intentions and actions.

As humans, we are constantly visualizing, or imagining, our past, present, and future. Daydreams, night dreams, meditations, and our millions of thoughts, contain a form of visualization. It is a normal part of who we are and how we are made. Whether you use visualization to manifest or to support affirmations, it is important that you visualize yourself actively pursuing your goals, not just achieving them.

Intentional visualization is not dreaming. It is not hoping and wishing. It is using your mind's eye to see yourself taking the specific steps needed to move you toward the life you deserve.

Often, the process of visualization is misunderstood. You can't just dream of yourself sailing around on a yacht, drinking champagne, rubbing shoulders with celebrities. Instead, it's about truly visualizing yourself taking the necessary actions to get there. It's about the process and the excitement of the journey.

Visualization builds on the foundation of previous chapters – speaking affirmations, setting intentions, maintaining a high frequency, and taking inspired action. Only after you grasp the meaning of those concepts will you understand what to visualize and how to manifest it into reality.

I discovered the effects of visualization by accident when I was on a weight loss journey. Each night before I fell asleep, I would visualize every single workout I was going to perform in the gym the next day. I walked myself through each exercise, down to each individual rep. I felt the pain of the weights and the difficulty of lifting heavy. I imagined every single movement. Little did I know that I was actually creating my new reality through visualization! My only intent was to practice a little bit in my head so I wouldn't be afraid when I got started in the gym the next morning.

Visualizing my workouts motivated me to wake up at 5:00 am each day to meet my trainer. This practice was instrumental in my weight loss journey, helping me to shed 82 pounds in just seven months. By envisioning myself achieving my fitness goals, I cultivated self-trust, inspired myself daily, and fostered fierce determination. I never anticipated the incredible fit transformation I would achieve, as there was no way I could imagine my true physical potential. Instead of envisioning my future body, which was uncertain to me, I focused on picturing the challenging exercises my trainer would have in store for me each morning.

You see, when you visualize, your brain doesn't know if what it's experiencing is real or not. Your mind feels and acts as if the actions you are taking are real, and our bodies have no choice but to respond. For instance, if you imagine biting into a lemon, what happens? Your body may react as if you're actually doing so, proving my point.

Combining visualization with your affirmations involves picturing in your mind what you are speaking. Imagine moving through your day with ease, feel how peaceful that feels, how easygoing your mood is. Imagine your presentation at work, everyone enjoying your words, praising your confidence and knowledge. Feel the success before, during, and after. Imagine yourself sitting down and writing your book, imagine every word and phrase going from your mind to your paper or computer. Imagine completing each chapter. Can you feel the pages as you turn them, reading your first published book? What does that feel like? Allow your visualization to be felt, heard, fully encompassing your brain, heart, and body.

When you imagine only the finish line, such as the celebration on the big yacht, you are leaving yourself with doubt. You are not proving to yourself that you have the means to get there. Now bear in mind, you may not know how you will get there. And that's okay. But you do know the next step. You do know what action to take next because you've been practicing the tools outlined in previous chapters. You've used affirmations "*I have clarity on the steps to take to propel me forward*", and "*I am in the exact place I'm meant to be.*" You've set your intentions for the day, you stay above the line in vibration, and you listen to your intuition on a regular basis. If you practice all these things, then you'll know what your next step is, no matter how small. And then you visualize and imagine yourself taking it. This is how you create your life on your own terms.

All these tools lay the foundation for you to create your reality. It's not magic or witchcraft, it's a scientific method to attract what you deserve. And you must believe that you deserve it!

Visualization is particularly useful when you need to work through challenging times. When facing fears or doubting your abilities, visualizing the result you want can help you see that anything is possible. Ask yourself *"What if things work out perfectly?"* Say out loud, *"Things are always working out for me!"* This mental rehearsal prepares you to handle difficult situations with ease, as you've already experienced them in your mind. Push through the resistance, that's where the magic happens.

There are no rules in imagining. The best part is you can do this process anyway you wish. Imagine you are on top of a mountain, overlooking an ocean, and all your fears are the big rocks, each one labeled and stacked up in front of you, blocking the gorgeous ocean view. Picture yourself removing these huge rocks one by one, and throwing them into the ocean. You say, "Goodbye fear of success," "Goodbye fear of failure," etc. Each time you see yourself throwing these blocks into the ocean, where they flow with the water far away from you until you can't see them anymore, you'll feel yourself becoming lighter. You'll be able to think clearer, and you'll attract the steps and actions you need to move forward toward your goals. Just one example of how you can use visualization to change your perspective.

Don't try to outsmart the universe! You must be authentic in all these processes, meaning be honest and truthful! Be sure your vision and your values line up! Define your success from your inner spirit, not from the flesh...meaning, don't use these tools for just THINGS. Your visualizations should include experiences with your family and friends, and encompass your life circumstances. What does your visualization mean to your life as a whole, not just as separate fleeting moments. We've all heard of celebrities having it all, but still feeling miserable...that's because they don't envision nor plan for what success actually brings. Superficial success can inadvertently attract unwanted problems. True abundance isn't just money or material possessions. Ask yourself what money brings to you - it's the joy, the freedom, the peace of mind, and stability that you really want. Think about that. If you had all the money in the world, ask yourself what part of that scenario would make you happy? Money and success are just worldly "things" we humans created that helps us get to the emotional place we dream of being. Once you take money out of the equation, and focus on the joy, stability, freedom, and carefree attitude, the money will flow right on in - all the way to your bank account.

Just as you may say "I want to lose weight," what that actually means might be:

"I feel good when I'm fit and strong."

"I love having the energy to do the activities I love."

"I love the way my clothes fit!"

Use reason statements and visuals to draw these blessings into your life.

You can use visualization exercises in many ways. Some like to create a story, like imagining physically handing over worries and fears to God. You can also visualize friends, family, even strangers, coming to help you. Picture yourself surrounded by these helpful people that want nothing but the best for you. Envision doors opening, opportunities arising, problems being solved out of the blue. Imagine the feelings of freedom and security those thoughts give you.

However you choose to use this exercise, it can help soothe away the pain and discomfort of doubt, fear, and discouragement.

We are all worthy of having everything we desire. As you practice visualization and affirmations, the key is to believe that you are worthy of receiving! Scientists say that the brain doesn't distinguish imagination or visualization from reality. Through imagining your wins, you can train your subconscious to replace fear and anxious thoughts.

Our past leaves us with unnecessary baggage, and this baggage is what prevents us from asking for the big things - you know, those things we only think about yet dare say out loud. You may not feel worthy of these things that you want to ask for. Someone may have told you that you weren't good enough, or smart enough to have such things like a prestigious job, or a bank account full of money, or the time to take a vacation. These are false beliefs that are embedded in us, and it's up to us to put in the effort to transform them out of our subconscious. Your story is yours to shape, so don't allow others to dictate it with their words or perspectives.

You must KNOW your blessings belong to you and that you are capable of receiving them. Sometimes, our sense of worthiness gets shaken by a little subconscious thought buried deep inside—a fear of change that whispers doubts. When you visualize yourself changing, transforming, trying new things, the fear goes *Poof*, and it's replaced by excitement and anticipation.

Fear acts as a barrier, blocking you from attracting what rightfully belongs to you. Sometimes, there's a misconception that being humble means not expecting or desiring great things. However, true humility lies in acknowledging your desires while maintaining a sense of gratitude. When you approach life with gratitude, you open the door to receiving all the things you want and more. This isn't just a coincidence—it's the universe responding to your positive energy and mindset.

Remember that inspired action we talked about? The action that comes from your intuition? You wouldn't have all of these ideas and blessings deep in your soul if you didn't deserve them. If God puts something in your soul, it's already yours! You just have to align with the energies to attract and receive them, and KNOW they belong to you! Inspired action is the way you show commitment to your goals, affirmations are the trust you have in those blessings, and visualization is proof of faith that you deserve them.

Self-love means treating yourself to what you truly deserve and taking care of yourself to build the life you're absolutely worthy of living. Affirmations are your acknowledgement of having those things, and visualization is showing your mind and body that these things are possible. Claim what you desire. If God put it in your heart, then it's already done!

Spend each moment savoring the good things in your environment. When you savor the good, and really attune your energy to them, it creates more images that you can use to visualize when you aren't feeling your best self. You can reflect on those memories and pull up those mental images to help get you back above the line. When you take the time to practice these self-love processes, your future self will always thank you!

When I was on my weight loss journey, I would have to face decisions about eating every second of the day. I was a junk food junkie, with 3 kids, constantly surrounded by snacks, candy, fast food, and bread! After months of making one healthy choice after another, I started each morning by thanking myself as I saw those smaller numbers on the scale. I'd literally say out loud, "Thank you for making the right choice yesterday!" It was the complete opposite of regret—it was gratitude. Gratitude to myself for being strong and for making the right choices. That wonderful feeling of joy, knowing I was doing this all FOR MYSELF, would carry me right through the evening, making it even easier to keep making those healthy choices.

This became a visualization I relied on when I was having a tough moment. Maybe the scale didn't move like I wanted, maybe I didn't want to go workout, whatever the case may be. I visualized the joy, happiness, gratitude of seeing the scale's new number tomorrow, and knew my future self would not be happy if I didn't do what she needed me to do. That got me up and moving. It also created more joy, happiness, and gratitude by default.

I know that weight loss isn't as serious an issue compared to dealing with things such as heartbreak, grief, financial loss, etc. But it's a true example of how you can use this practice and how you may be already doing it without knowing!

Visualization creates movement. It tells our minds we are ready to do what it takes to achieve our goals and dreams. Before God created the heavens and the earth he had a vision in mind. Before anything became reality, someone, somewhere, thought about it. Had an idea. A thought. A dream. A vision. No where at all in history or science exists an idea formed without a visual representation of it.

So, get daydreaming!

♥

"I see opportunities for growth in every challenge."

"I see the beauty within myself and others."

"I trust in the process and believe in my vision."

"I visualize success and it becomes my reality."

"I am aligned with the energy of love, peace, and happiness."

"Things are always working out for me."

"I am safe and successful."

"I have everything I need and my needs are always provided for through my positive words."

"I am worthy of all the good things I envision for myself."

"I see myself achieving my goals with clarity and confidence."

"I know exactly what I want."

MY AFFIRMATIONS WORKSHEET

CHAPTER 7

Mindfulness and Acceptance

"Be careful how you think; your life is shaped by your thoughts."

Proverbs 4:23

Have you ever heard someone tell you to "Live in the moment"? It's a piece of advice that's as old as time, echoing through countless spiritual teachings, age-old philosophies, and even modern psychological practices. They all sing the same tune about the sweet rewards of staying in the present.

Imagine a quiet morning on the porch with nothing but the sound of the birds and a gentle breeze, while you soak up every bit of peace - that's living in the moment. It's about not letting your mind wander to the grocery list or the dust on the mantle, but instead, really being right there, feeling the warmth of the breeze and deciphering the chirps of the birds. Let me tell you, there's a ton of good that comes from embracing the here and now, and that's what we're going to dive into in this chapter.

But what if you're a worrier? Or a Virgo, like me? I worry. I need to plan. I overthink even the smallest of things. The most difficult thing for me to do is to be present and accept the flexibility and flow of life. How can I rewire my brain to get off the wheel of overthinking and worrying?

Accepting our circumstances without judgment is just one result of practicing affirmations, visualization, and all the beautiful tools I've outlined in previous chapters. Acceptance is also being open to receiving, and accepting with a full heart, the multitude of blessings that you attract.

A few years back, someone complimented me on being a top-notch multitasker. I used to wear that label like a badge of honor, thinking it was one of my strong suits. Turns out, it was just a fancy way of saying I was always distracted, never fully here in the moment.

Nothing compares to the feeling when you can look back and see how much you've changed. Reflecting on the person I was years ago, I see the broken pieces that needed mending, and just how far I've come with nothing but my daily practices. Now, I'm more in tune with my emotions and I use my affirmations to sidestep those negative vibes. It's like watching the new me manage things the old me couldn't handle.

"I am worthy of all that I have."

"I am smart and capable to succeed in my career."

"I love having peace and beautiful things in my life."

I find it much easier now to pause, be still, and really listen to my intuition—which speaks up loud and clear throughout my day. Mindfulness can truly offer precious insights into your life, showing you not just who you are, but who you're meant to be around, and what you're meant to be doing.

When you practice mindfulness, you become more attuned to the beauty and blessings around you, fostering a deep sense of appreciation for the richness of life. These positive points of view literally change you. They transform you into a person capable of building the life you deserve.

One of my favorite mindful practices is something called "grounding." I take a few minutes each day, step outside into the grass barefoot, and allow my body to absorb the earth's energy while I clear my mind. It's simple and straightforward, and I always feel energized afterwards. There's plenty of benefits to grounding. If this interests you, why not take a few moments and do some research on how it can do you some good, too.

Mindfulness and acceptance mean recognizing the powerful spirit within you and understanding that your feelings and emotions are perfectly valid. It also means knowing that you have the power to change your mood and mindset at any moment. It's all about grasping the idea that you hold the reins to your future. Embracing the blessings you draw into your life is part of acceptance. From a simple compliment from a stranger to the profound, divine gifts you've prayed for. These blessings are meant for you. Don't dismiss them. Welcome them with open arms and be grateful that you've attracted them.

When you snag that parking spot right up front, when someone lets you cut ahead in line, when a kind soul holds the door for you, when you receive a compliment, or when someone treats you to a coffee or lends you a few bucks—believe it or not, you've had a hand in orchestrating all these little blessings. So, go ahead and embrace them! You've put these requests out into the universe. Once they come your way, be grateful and remember, you are absolutely worthy of these kindnesses.

When you accept where you are on your journey through life, and choose to embrace every waking moment, your life transforms. Sometimes we are in a difficult place in life. Sometimes we feel despair or anger. Be mindful of these feelings and use these processes to change the way you see and speak about them. It can and will positively affect your circumstance. When you practice mindfulness, you become more attuned to the beauty and blessings around you, fostering a deep sense of appreciation for the richness of life.

"No weapon formed against me will prosper."

"I am healthy."

"I am blessed."

The best thing about life is that it's constantly changing. I used to absolutely hate change. Mostly, because change forces me to face the unknown. Remember that fear we talked about in an earlier chapter? We are all afraid of the dark in some way. Learning to let go of outcomes and live in each moment on our journey is where the magic happens. Be open to things working out for you! Every time we face the day with appreciation, excitement, and anticipation, more of the magic is attracted. And when we are in an incredibly low point in life, we must remember tomorrow is another day.

"Everyday is a new day."

"This too shall pass."

"I'm surrounded by love and support at all times."

Repeating affirmations for navigating through situations that feel tough or are pain points during your day leads your mind to see the good in everything. This is a habit that fights against everything we've known from childhood. When we are in pain, we cry. When we suffer, we feel bad. Changing this habit, reaching for a new perspective is just like going to the gym and strengthening our muscles. It takes a lot of practice. But each time you choose faith over fear, you move closer to your ideal reality. This type of mindset can create a more receptive environment for manifesting positive changes.

Now I know, we aren't robots. There are times when we fall way below the line. Doubt creeps in. Pain returns. We are exhausted. We wake up and think we cannot make it even one more day. But guess what - we do! The quicker you train your mind to intercept these moments, the faster you start focusing on the affirmations you have written on notepads and sticky notes all around the house, the easier it will be to get out of bed and tackle the day with even a smidgen of enthusiasm. You will make it to the next day. And oh, what great opportunities are arriving soon!

If you start to slip off a ladder, catching yourself right there on that first step down makes regaining your balance a whole lot easier. If you tumble all the way to the bottom, well, pulling yourself back up is going to be much tougher. Be mindful of your energy. Be mindful of the negative thoughts creeping in. You only need one doubt, one fear, one small dip below the line, and boom - here comes the enemy ready to pounce and ruin your day.

Incorporating mindfulness into your daily life doesn't necessarily require deep meditation or yoga sessions; it can be woven into your routine seamlessly. *"I can do this," "God's got me"*. As easy as incorporating affirmations into your daily life, mindfulness acts as it's best friend, speeding up the process of bestowing divine favors all over you. Be open to receiving all that's meant for you.

When I started realizing I was using the above the line analogy, it was because I was using mindfulness to catch myself talking negative about someone, damning to hell my circumstances, swearing, getting angry, upset, or anxious. I'd literally say out loud "Ok, stop. Stay above the line." And I'd switch my thoughts and focus on purpose on something entirely different.

"Reckless words pierce like a sword, but the tongue of the wise brings healing." (Proverbs 12:18)

Whenever I'd experience rough patches, I'd turn to my backyard porch. Swinging from my hammock outside in ridiculously hot and humid weather, my Louisiana backyard became my safe haven for practicing mindfulness. My mind would race with fearful "what if" thoughts. I had heard about refocusing during what I'd call a panic attack, so I practiced changing my pattern of thinking. I'd take a deep breath and push out all of the negative feelings, while at the same time, listening to any sound within earshot. Usually, there were crickets, frogs, maybe some birds, a little traffic, an air conditioning running. The more I listened, the more sounds I would recognize. Sometimes the insects would chirp and the frogs would croak in unison, creating a nighttime or daytime rhythmic song. After a few minutes of listening, trying to make sense of the calmness of these intrusive sounds, I'd be in a much better state of mind. My thoughts would stop spiraling, a sense of relief would come over me as new thoughts occupied my mind such as:

"Things are changing for the better."

"I don't have to figure it all out now, things are always brighter in the mornings."

I changed the negative "What If" statements to positive ones:

"What if everything works out better than I can imagine?"

"What if this leads me to something great?"

The simplest way to explain mindfulness is to just be present. Be where you are when you are there. Look at your surroundings. Listen to your environment. Stop and smell the roses! (Cliché, but it works!)

That's exactly why I picked a dandelion for the cover of this book—it reminds us of all the desires we hold that have yet to come to pass. Have you ever leaned in, whispered your wishes to a dandelion, and watched its seeds sail away into the breeze?

Back when I was living in Tennessee, come springtime, I was amazed by the number of dandelions that covered the yards. I'd snap pictures, pick a few, and scatter their seeds with a gentle breath. Each time, it offered me a much-needed pause—a few quiet moments to reflect on what I truly wanted and to appreciate the simple beauty of a tiny flower. What a perfect reminder to open our hearts to believing all things are working out for us.

When you're on the phone, truly listen to the person on the other end of the call. And if you're having coffee with a friend, tuck that phone away. You never know—this might be the moment you hear a bit of news that answers a question or gives you just the solution you've been needing, like finding a pearl in an oyster when you least expect it.

You know what else I find to be grounding and mindful? A farmer's market! It's a great place to practice mindfulness as you fully immerse yourself in the sights and sounds. When you go to a farmer's market, it's like stepping into a lively, colorful world of fresh produce and homemade goods. You're greeted with the smell of ripe fruits, freshly baked bread, and herbs. You might sample fresh berries or sip on homemade lemonade while chatting with vendors about their products. It's a mindful experience that connects you to the local land and the people who work it. You leave feeling grounded and appreciative of the simple joys in life, which lands you in a higher vibration.

Remember to be present of your self-talk, the thoughts and words you tell yourself and others. What thoughts are you allowing to fester in your mind? Is it fear? Doubt? Anger? Disappointment? Or is it Hope? Love? Confidence? Anticipation? Faith? There's no room for living both above and below the line. You've got to choose, moment by moment, what you'll focus on. You decide what thoughts you'll let take up space in your mind and what your life will look like come morning. It's all in your hands.

What will your future self be thankful for?

When good things happen, stop and express gratitude for those moments, no matter how big or small they may be. *"Yes! I'm so thankful for that green light so I can make it work on time!"* and *"So happy I made it through that meeting"*. These statements get the good energy moving and swirling all around you!

Anytime you feel your mind wandering, call it back to the present by feeling the objects in your hands, paying attention to body sensations, listen to sounds around you. Sometimes I will sing aloud, making up songs about what I am doing just to keep me focused on the present. This keeps my anxiety and my active mind at bay. Whatever it takes, do it, because it sure feels better living in a good mood rather than a bad one.

Things are always working out for us. We must firmly believe this and live it every day regardless of our circumstances. That's another part of the acceptance.

"*I know this is going to change for the better.*"

"*I am learning from this experience that will soon be over.*"

There is a passage in the bible that says, **"When I am afraid, I put my trust in you." (Psalm 56:3).** When you put trust in God, the universe will never lead us astray. It is our own human thinking and un-inspired action that creates conflict.

When I was in the midst of Hurricane Katrina, homeless, with three small children, no hope in sight, the song "Be Not Afraid" was sung during mass at church. I cried right there surrounded by the congregation, and I didn't care. The overwhelming feeling of appreciation and hope, and most importantly RELIEF, took over from pain and despair, flowing through my body, and I remembered there's always something to hold onto when we are drowning. I accepted my situation and knew that this was just something I had to endure. And it wouldn't last forever. Just one part of one chapter in the story of my life.

Acceptance can help relieve pain and suffering.

"*I accept this part of my life and eagerly await my new chapters.*"

"*I know this is temporary.*"

"*I know that everything works out for me.*"

"*I am exactly where I'm meant to be at this moment.*"

Sometimes I have to say this 100 times in a day before I can feel it and believe it. It takes some time to outsmart that genius brain we have, but eventually it will become easier.

You can use affirmations so easily during mindful moments. They start to come to you without thinking. These words will brick the path for your future steps. Say them out loud as you wander through your day.

By staying grounded in the present, your appreciation for the beauty of life will grow.

♥

"*I embrace this task with gratitude.*"

"*I am grateful for a house that offers me peace and love.*"

"*I am grateful for the food I feed to myself and my family.*"

"*I savor the beauty of my surroundings.*"

"I appreciate my body and its unlimited capabilities."

"I know every moment of my life is uniquely special."

"I feel excited to attract everything I desire with ease."

"I am capable of staying fit and healthy."

"The cells in my body know how to keep me fit and strong."

"I accept and receive the blessings that are attracted to me."

"I feel joy in all that I do."

"I am grateful and eager for new opportunities."

MY AFFIRMATIONS WORKSHEET

CHAPTER 8

‘‘

Trusting Your Power

**"And whatever you ask in prayer, you will receive,
if you have faith."**

Matthew 21:22

As the verse says: What we ask for, we will receive. Such a weighty and complex idea – or is it just that simple? As the Scriptures say, we can trust God and know that all the blessings He graces us with will be realized. But what about trusting in the path we are walking today?

What does it mean to trust in ourselves?

An easy definition - Trusting yourself means having confidence in your own judgments, decisions, and capabilities. It involves listening to and honoring your inner voice, recognizing your intuition, and acting based on what feels right for you, even in the face of doubt or opposition from others.

Is trust confidence? Worthiness? Faith?

Trust isn't simply believing that you are the director of your life, but rather that you have faith in your ability to interpret and utilize the tools you were endowed with at birth, to shape your life.

In other words, you must trust your intuition. Trust your gut. Trust your decisions. Trust that you are where you are meant to be. Trust your path. Trust the process. Trust God. Trust the Universe has your back! Trust your beliefs.

We use the word trust to describe our trust in people, our trust in objects, our trust in processes, all external things. But to trust in a higher power, such as God, requires serious vulnerability, and to trust yourself, well, that is even harder.

We grow up learning to trust what others teach us. We are born with the tools to discern between right and wrong, good and bad. Our instincts evolve as does our knowledge and habits. Yet, turning our attention inward often slips from our priorities. We start trusting externally and forget how to trust our instincts and intuition.

This is the age of self-love. Self-expression. Self-indulgence. But somewhere all these things get lost in translation amid real life.

Now, bear in mind, trusting yourself doesn't mean acting out and doing what's best for you without taking into consideration love, respect, compassion, integrity, and honesty. It is, instead, quieting your mind, centering yourself and listening to an inner voice that's so much bigger than you, tapping into those quiet messages that are smothered by the day to day lives we live.

Your affirmations will only work if you trust them. If you trust yourself. If you believe what you are saying. You must believe to receive! If you recognize and acknowledge your deepest feelings and TRUST that things are always working out for you. And above all, trust that God is working for your good, even if you can't see a way out, there is one.

You know that little voice that always says, "There's no way this will work out." That's you, not trusting yourself. That's the voice of doubt and fear. Don't doubt your destiny. Trust that you are always doing what's best for you at this moment. Trust that you are on the right path. Trust that you can instinctively navigate through your weaknesses and strengths and recognize the difference.

Learn to make promises to yourself that you will keep. I realized that every time I lie to myself, I am eroding my self-trust, fostering self-doubt and self-hatred. Every morning, I tell myself I'm going to the gym. I make promises the night before, set my alarm, pick out my clothes, and plan to go. But the next day, I don't follow through. Sound familiar?

We do this all the time. "Today, I'm going to call my friend." "Tomorrow, I'm going to go grocery shopping." It's a daily habit, we make promises to ourselves and then we don't follow through.

I thought about this enough to realize I needed to change this habit. I made so many promises that I began to lose all trust in myself. So much that it affected my decision making and caused me to feel a ton of regret. I also would feel guilty and speak negatively to myself at the end of the day, subconsciously punishing myself for not doing what I promised I would do. What a cycle of self-abuse!

Let's break it down. Why do I need to go to the gym? Ok, maybe I need to move around more? Maybe I need to get out of the house. Maybe I need to lose some weight. All of that can be accomplished in many other ways besides JUST going to the gym. So now I say *"Today, I'm going to get moving."* This could mean listening to loud music and dancing. It could be walking my dogs an extra block. It could be working in the garden, pulling weeds, or mowing the yard. When you act from a place of honesty and trust, by the day's end, you're likely to feel a surge of positive energy and gratitude. Often, it's those little steps that actually propel us toward our goals much quicker.

This is crucial. We're talking about reversing self-sabotage and self-abuse here. We need to learn to extend grace and compassion to ourselves. Pay attention to that inner voice that assures us we deserve love and honor, not disgrace. It's about creating a space where our hearts, minds, and souls feel trusted and respected, preventing us from directing our frustrations at ourselves or others. Affirm to yourself, *"I trust I am doing what's right for me."*

Our brain and bodies are always picking up signals or messages, telling us what to do and what not to do. We can hear this divine guidance by listening to our inner self. These messages come to us in the form of a gut feeling or red flags. Our intuition helps to translate these messages, but we must learn to trust enough to act upon what we begin to know.

Sometimes, you will see evidence that will strengthen the trust in yourself, this process, and the universe or God. It can be as simple as following the tiny road maps that lead you to where you need to be.

Once, I was struggling with poor lighting while working at my computer. Sitting by an open window caused too many shadows, and the overhead lights just weren't cutting it. I briefly considered buying one of those circle lights popular with influencers, but I shrugged off the idea. A few days later, on a whim, I popped into one of my favorite stores for some retail therapy. To my surprise, the store was closing down and everything was half off! It was my go-to place for home decor, so I grabbed a cart and started loading up. At the checkout, the clerk unexpectedly pointed to a circle light, priced at just $1, and said it was the last one left. That moment was a perfect example of the universe nudging us with hidden messages, and I followed through by taking the inspired action. I couldn't help but laugh as I added the light to my cart, thankful for the universe's perfect timing.

Even this simple story of success is a reminder of how trusting ourselves and following the universe's guidance can lead us in the right direction.

Trust can be a misguided notion of always believing in the positive. The key to this is that you aren't just believing, you are actually <u>creating</u>. To some, it can be easy to believe that positive things are going to happen. And we all know that things are always changing. But trusting your own inner guidance to actually MAKE those things happen, to align with the right frequency to create your world, and design the life you want - that's the challenge.

When you start to trust yourself, it's not all unicorns and rainbows. You must first move through the feelings of self-doubt, anxiety, and insecurity, living among your thoughts. The biggest of these negative liars is once again, fear. We already know that fear can paralyze you into thinking negatively and keeps you from anything and everything that you desire. Fear will take you down at the knees and keep you from experiencing life in every way, shape, and form. Fear can be very powerful, but now you have the antidote - Trust. Trust is saying to fear "I hear you, but I trust that everything is working out for me."

Trust your instincts. Trust your gut. Trust in your complete wholeness of who you are. Trust in your ability to change your future, create your life and design the environment in which you live. All of this is possible. Repeat affirmations such as:

"I trust myself."

"I trust in the Lord."

"I trust things are always working out for me."

"I trust the unfolding of my journey."

We trust the sun will rise. We trust the sun will set. We set our alarms at night because we trust we will wake up the next day. We make vacation plans because we trust we will live long enough to enjoy them. We trust the birds will sing and they, in turn, trust they will find food and shelter. Just watch how animals live from season to season. They trust they have all that they need. They trust that the world is created for them. We should be so lucky to live in their uncomplicated way of thinking.

Trust and belief go hand in hand. Trusting yourself is key. We all have everything we need deep inside of us. Our heart and head provide information for us to use to make decisions. Many times, we say they battle one another. But the heart is our soul, our

131

inner knowing. Our head is the brain that tries to humanly interpret those feelings, and sometimes, it can be wrong. This is the most important part of trust. To stop, listen, and open your mind to what the heart is telling you. Trust your gut that is leading you on your best path.

When things look bleak, we must remember to control that inner dialogue. With each positive step forward, your path begins to light up. You start to see clarity in your thoughts. We don't have to figure everything out right now. We just need to keep stepping forward, following the cues our bodies give us. God's the one lighting our path, after all. Picture yourself walking along a path, and with each step you take, it lights up right under your feet. It's as if each move forward is guided by a little divine spark.

Sometimes, if we saw the entire road ahead it would look daunting or overwhelming and we wouldn't even take the first step. But when you take small steps, even tiny ones, it seems much easier to conquer. I recall a colleague who often said: How do you eat an elephant? One bite at a time.

Every journey begins with one step. I use this trick each day to move forward. Every day is a new day, meaning just handle what is in front of you, the present, and your future will fall into place. It is not our job to control the future. But we can design our life by knowing and believing the steps we take today, the decisions we make right now in the present, sets our course for the future.

During my fitness journey, I faced constant decisions about what to eat. I needed to stop indulging in unhealthy food and start choosing healthier options. That meant no more junk food, skipping the popcorn at the movies, and doing all this while my kids were munching on snacks around me all day.

"I am capable of eating healthy."

"The food I eat nurtures my body and builds muscles."

"I am grateful for the healthy food that I eat."

I realized when I trusted myself to make the right choices, my future self would thank me, and I learned to trust myself even more.

Each time I recognize an intuitive message, I make sure to take the inspired action that follows. The more you on these tiny nudges instead of ignoring them, the more you learn to trust yourself.

I learned to trust myself to make the choices best for me. I didn't let myself down. I used affirmations to keep myself moving forward and surrounded with good energy.

I once tackled a half-marathon with zero training—yeah, I'm laughing as I type this because, goodness, it was a wild idea. I ran alongside a group of coworkers who thought I'd lost my marbles but cheered me on all the same. In my head, I broke it down really simple: I knew I could jog a solid two miles without stopping, figured with a bit more determination I could stretch that to four. Then, I thought, why not push it to eight? I figured that's about when I'd be ready to throw in the towel, so I'd likely slow to a walk around mile nine or ten. After that, it was just about mustering whatever I had left to cross that finish line. I set the intention to finish this long run. I visualized myself at each mile. I trusted my body would cooperate.

Guess what? I finished the half-marathon and crossed the finish line averaging an 11-minute mile.

I had absolute faith in myself to pull it off. I just knew I could make it happen. Doubt never crossed my mind. I didn't physically prepare; I wasn't scared of the hurt. I just told myself, "We're gonna do this," and then I went out and did something I'd never dream of doing (and by the way, will never, ever do again)!

As humans, we can adapt and shift our paths to create the best life possible for ourselves. We can point ourselves in a positive direction with our power of choice. Trusting ourselves involves recognizing when we need to step outside of our comfort zone and change course. Affirmations can help us stay above the line while we do just that.

♥

"I trust that I am on my right path."

"I trust that I am where I am supposed to be."

"I feel confident in my decisions."

"I hear the messages from my intuition."

"I have clarity in everything I do."

"I am capable of making the right choices."

"I know I am growing stronger every day."

"I am free of all self-doubt about myself and my work."

"God has a plan for my life, and I hear his messages."

"I am thankful for my ability to trust myself."

"I have the strength encourage to overcome any challenge."

"I am amazing and can do amazing things."

MY AFFIRMATIONS WORKSHEET

CHAPTER 9

Vvvvvvvvvvvvvvvvvvvvvvvvvvvvvvvvvvvvvvvvvvvvvvvvv

Glimpses and Inklings

"And in the last days, God says, 'I will pour out my Spirit on all people. Your sons and daughters will prophesy, your young men will see visions, your old men will dream dreams.'"

Acts 2:17

You might've heard of the terms 'Glimpses' and 'Glimmers.' These are words that can explain when you get that feeling of déjà vu, or when, for a fleeting second, you sense something absolutely wonderful is on the horizon. I sometimes call these sweet moments 'inklings', because I picture them like little filaments of energy floating in and out of my surroundings.

A 'glimpse' is like peering through a window into your future, catching sight of what might be coming down the pike. An 'inkling,' on the other hand, is that familiar feeling of déjà vu, or that tickle in your spirit telling you something good's about to unfold. Whenever you feel this, stop and recognize the feeling, and say "*Ooooohhh, this is going to be good!*"

I find myself catching glimpses and feeling inklings quite often. They tend to pop up at the oddest times, usually when your mind is as clear as a bell and wide open to whatever messages the good Lord is sending your way. Sometimes, it's when I get in my car and right before I put my foot on the gas to make it go. That slight pause, when your mind completely empties, and your body takes over. That fleeting moment allows a glimpse or inkling to be received. Sometimes, it's when I'm walking outside or soaking in a hot bath. These little assurances that blessings are around the bend are just waiting for us to stretch out our hands and grab hold.

But here's the thing about inklings and glimpses—they're the polar opposite of triggers. Where a trigger might make you put up your defenses because it stirs up fear or pain, an inkling does just the opposite—it fills you with joy and peace, and might even coax a smile out of you.

Inklings are so brief, fleeting like a firefly on a summer night, that before you know it, they've slipped through your fingers. Our busy brains often snap us right back to the here and now before we've had a chance to really savor that moment of grace. It takes a bit of practice to let these precious moments linger a tad longer.

And glimpses? Well, they're just about as contrary to focus as you can get. The moment you try to pin down what your heart and soul are showing you, poof—it vanishes. That's because a glimpse isn't born from the mind or the ego; it comes from deeper within—from your energy, your heart, your very spirit.

You can't hold onto it; it's not something you can touch. It's temporary, like a fairy angel flitting past your eyes, and just as soon as you blink, it's gone.

But oh, honey, it's a glimpse into the life you're meant to lead.

Think about a time when you thought "I'm meant to have a better life" or "I feel like I should have been a doctor, lawyer, teacher, hiker, swimmer," etc. Sometimes I use the term "past life" as in saying "I feel like I've done this in a past life." My guess is that it wasn't in a past life, it's in the life I'm meant to have. A life that is right there at the edge, waiting for me to rise to the appropriate frequency to gain access to its blessings.

Glimpses are simply messages from your spirit that nudge you and tell you to go explore these thoughts. Sometimes, they aren't specific at all, but you just get 'a feeling' that there is something you need to figure out.

Imagine you've been feeling unsure about a decision regarding booking an expensive vacation. You've meditated, prayed, and asked the Universe for guidance, aiming to align your thoughts with what you truly desire. Is the timing right? Should I spend the money? Am I being selfish?

One day, while working in your garden, you suddenly feel a profound sense of peace while picturing a mental image of yourself joyfully on this vacation. This unexpected moment of clarity and joy, which aligns perfectly with your inner desires and the vibrations you've been focusing on, is a spiritual glimpse. It's last no more than a split second. It serves as a sign from the Universe, God, and your angels that you are on the right path and that your alignment with your true self is attracting what you desire into your life.

The first time I set foot in Tennessee was on a family vacation. Oh, the country air, the majestic mountains, and that pure, clean energy—it just called out to me. It's energy spoke to my spirit. Fast forward ten years, and wouldn't you know it, my son got accepted to the University of Tennessee-Chattanooga. That's where he met his darling wife, and now they've set up their home near there. I visited often, and with each visit, I'd experience little glimpses of a life where I lived there, and it became more frequent.

About three years later, I landed a job in Nashville. Not long after I settled in, I found myself exploring a quaint small town on the outskirts. As I drove down Main Street, I experienced a glimpse of myself calling this town home. As I was driving, soaking it all in, I said out loud, "I will live here someday." And would you believe it? A year to the day, I moved into a house right in that very town. It wasn't until I was unpacking, taking in the beauty and the special feel of my new place, that it hit me—I had declared this move a year ago! And there I was, living the very dream I'd once spoken into existence, catching a glimpse of it long before it ever came to be.

This is how we experience glimpses and inklings that support our affirmations, and are proof of our manifestations. They help us feel the energy of where we are meant to be, our future. So, we can tune in to our intuition, speak our desires, visualize our happiness and joy, and all those things help get us there. It's creating our life! It's building the life we want.

You see, we come to this earth already knowing what our purpose is: where we need to go, where we need to be, and what we need to do to fulfill that purpose. The whole mission of being human is to learn as we move along our journey. We are students of this life, and learning to use the tools provided to us makes life easy. Glimpses and inklings can show us all the possibilities provided to us if we are paying attention.

I frequently have glimpses of myself standing on a stage speaking to others. I also have glimpses and inklings of writing and reading books to others. I know I'm meant to share my stories and help others. It took me a long time to learn how to trust the process, the journeys, and how to take one step at a time. Maybe I wasn't yet fully ready to receive my blessings. Maybe I wasn't wide open to receive my guidance. Whenever someone would say 'you should write a book' I'd say, 'Yea I know'. And that was the end of it.

I feel my best when I'm chattin' away. There's just something about speaking to a group of people that fills me with joy and happiness. The sharing of my thoughts and connecting with others through words - it's a feeling deep down in my soul that brings me peace. If it's a presentation, I often don't even plan what I'm going to say. I just allow the words just flow right out. If it's with friends and family, they have to hang up on me to get me to shut up. But, I know deep down it's my calling, and I'm getting better at listening to those little nudges, paying attention to those brief glimpses, and tuning into the energy that guides me.

"I am always speaking the words that others are meant to hear."

"I trust myself to speak the right words at the right time."

Sometimes, my inklings are so strong, they make me giggle. Once, when I was on a solo trip to Sedona, Arizona, I stopped dead in my tracks. While attempting to cross a busy street, I recognized an inkling where I felt I had experienced this moment before. I remember muttering something about how I didn't know what is or will be, but then I thought, "I sure can't wait to find out what this means."

Had I not understood what glimpses and inklings were, I would have just thought it was deja'vu or looked like a place I had already been. I would have dismissed the inkling instead of paying attention to it. That day confirmed I was living my manifestation of a perfect solo vacation in the desert.

"I am grateful I am on the right path."

"I trust my journey."

"I am open to new opportunities."

These strange or weird things happen to all of us often. The kick is – they aren't strange and definitely not weird to those of you reading this book. You will experience glimpses, nudges, inklings, and manifestations daily. Maybe even minute by minute. It is up to us to learn how to recognize them and use their wisdom to continue to build the life we deserve.

We can even catch those glimpses or inklings during demanding times, or when we're knee-deep in something tough. It

143

can be just a brief moment of relief, like suddenly forgetting all the heavy stuff you're going through. Maybe laughing for a just a second, or smiling at the thought of a beautiful memory. But then, sure as the world exists, the dread and doom come creeping back in. These little moments are meant to push us forward, to remind us that this rough patch won't last forever. It's a sign that we're moving through the thick of it, and brighter days are just within our reach. Speak your affirmations and solidify the creation of the life you want.

Glimpses and inklings are signs that our manifestations are taking shape. They're the physical realizations of our desires, the energy of our dreams forming around us, making us see a vision or feel a sensation. When these moments happen, take it as a sign that you're definitely on the right path.

You can engage with these images and feelings, just as if they are fluid thoughts and daydreams. Ask yourself what they might mean or represent. They are meant to teach you something or show you the path forward.

I always express affirmations of gratitude after experiencing inklings or glimpses. Sometimes, I ask for clarity.

"Thank you for showing me all things are possible."

"I appreciate glimpses that show me the right path forward."

Have an open heart and mind. You never know what your spirit may show you.

"I trust the message I receive from my intuition."

"I am a magnet for all good things."

"I am open and receptive to divine guidance and intuition."

"I trust in the subtle signs that guide my decisions & actions."

"My path is lit by the clear light of intuition, and I walk it with trust."

"I am aligned with my deepest insights, and I trust them."

"I am grateful for divine guidance."

"Thank you for showing me the path forward."

"I walk by grace and God's favor."

"I am a powerful connector to my purpose."

MY AFFIRMATIONS WORKSHEET

CHAPTER 10

~~~~~~

Gratitude

"Since everything God created is good, we should not reject any of it but receive it with thanks. For we know it is made acceptable by the word of God and prayer."

Timothy 4: 4-5

I am most excited about writing this chapter. I think I saved the best for last. If you take away nothing else from this book, let it be this chapter.

Understand that gratitude and appreciation can have profound changes on your life. It is sometimes the missing piece of the puzzle, and when put in place, completes the process of creating your life.

There are so many things to be thankful for. The key is to find appreciation in every single moment of our lives. And then voice that gratitude out loud.

I am profoundly grateful that I was able to write this book. I appreciate the words that inspired me. I am thankful for the laptop and cozy chair I used to put them together for you.

I am thankful for every person that reads this book. I am grateful for the inspiration to write the words that appeared in my mind throughout the day and during my dreams. It is most often that our greatest victories come after our biggest challenges. I am so appreciative of all the challenges I've experienced so that I could write these stories for you to read.

When you start a practice of gratitude, the grass looks greener, the trees fuller, the birds harmonize better, and you can hear whispers of blessings in everything you do. It opens the part of your brain that increases feelings of happiness and well-being. It strengthens your connections with others.

Gratitude rises your frequency to the level of abundance.

Notice that the quote that I chose to represent this chapter uses the term *"receive it with thanks."* You can decipher this phrase many different ways.

How many times would you give someone a gift without receiving a "thank you" in return?

Probably not many.

You see, we want to be sure that someone is thankful for the little bits of joy that we may bring into their lives. We want to know that we are blessing them with the right things, in the right way. That's how I picture our relationship with God and the universe.

When we acknowledge our blessings and gifts that are given to us, in turn, we receive more of them! We are meant to experience all the goodness created for us, allowing us to co-create and design our lives. Maintaining a grateful mindset keeps all that positive energy circulating. Living in an appreciative state signals the universe "More of this, More of that!"

Another way I see this phrase is as a gentle reminder to be thankful for everything, even the parts of life that aren't quite perfect. Accept your blessings, accept God's favor, even when they come wrapped in challenges or a bit of difficulty. It's all about seeing each moment as a chance to grow and learn, helping us to stand a little stronger and trust a little deeper, no matter what life throws our way.

Learn to accept and receive compliments, gifts, help and support from others, often in ways that might seem unexpected. Express gratitude to those who give to you and recognize that you are deserving of all the things that enhance your positive energy! Acknowledge their generosity, and remember, accepting these gifts and support confidently affirms your worthiness and contributes to a cycle of positive energy and goodwill

And it lifts others' spirits too. Don't rob someone of a feel-good moment—recognize their kindness.

Using gratitude in affirmations is the easiest way to stay above the line, giving you access to whatever you need at any given time. Appreciate the car you get to drive to work, feel grateful you have a job, and be thankful that you collaborate with other like-minded people. Be appreciative you'll move to bigger and better opportunities when the time is right.

"Thank you for the confidence to face each day with grace."

"I am grateful things around me become better each day."

When I spent almost a year unemployed, struggling to find a job, being misguided and rejected on a daily basis, I felt defeated. I could have stayed in bed under the covers each day, but I had to pull myself out of the funk and remind myself of the beauty in my life. I would wake up each morning and say, *"Thank you for the ability to find a new job."* Sometimes I'd say, *"Thank you for allowing that person to reject me so I can find a job that's perfect for me."* I'd state my affirmations daily around the job I wanted. *"I know I am on my way to a job that respects me and values my experience."* I'd even use that sentence in my interviews and job applications.

Yes, I did find a new job - one that respects me, values my input and experience, and allows me the flexibility to live my life on my terms. I know for a fact that I would have ended up in a different situation had I not used affirmations and gratitude to attract new opportunities. I know my affirmations and positive mindset, along with living graciously, helped me through the learning process of an unemployment journey.

What journey could you have lived differently?

Looking back, it feels as if it never happened, because I did my best to live every moment of each day and stay above the line. It was a blip on my life's history, full of positive and glorious days spent enjoying my temporary free time.

I am thankful that Hurricane Katrina changed my life, and transformed me into the person I am today. What could be a sad story, a depressing memory, lives in my mind with so many lessons and blessings it bestowed on me. While it is still a terrible experience, I no longer feel anxiety, anger, or sadness when I tell the story. It is now a story of resilience, wrapped up in gratitude that we made it through.

Each day I walk into my home, I state out loud *"I love my house. Thank you for this beautiful home."* It changes the energy. It changes my mood. And when others walk into my home, they say "Wow, your house smells so good." It's not just a scent, it's the energy I carry, and I do my best to maintain it. My home is my safe haven, and I treat it as such. I speak words of affirmation all day everyday. I appreciate my home, the sky, the weather (even when it's brutally hot and humid here in Louisiana). I walk around my home as I'm cleaning and I say words of gratitude about everything:

"I love these countertops."

"I love my backyard view."

"I am excited to decorate this house."

"I am grateful for my neighbors."

None of this is difficult to understand. It's literally noticing the good things in your life to demonstrate that you are ready to receive more of them.

Gratitude really shifts the way we see things. Ever tried feeling thankful and mad at the same time? It just doesn't mix. Gratitude's that stronger feeling that takes over as the dominant emotion. Whenever those negative thoughts start creeping in, I toss in a few thankful thoughts to lift me back up right away.

It's like popping on those rose-colored glasses. Only, you're not ignoring what's going on around you; you're just choosing to zero in on the good stuff. And let me tell you, the good stuff sure feels a whole lot better.

Feel grateful for those that are in your life. Like really *feel* grateful for them. Focus on their best attributes. Practice gratitude to your circle of friends and appreciate all they do to support you or what they bring to your life.

Gratitude fosters forgiveness and empathy, which brings us closer to love and compassion.

When you watch your friends receive blessings, declare your gratitude! When you see others manifesting their success, feel excited that this is possible for you, too. Support them in the way you would want to be supported.

As you start incorporating the practices outlined in this book, you'll begin to see blessings and abundance flourishing around the people close to you as well. Your energy influences their energy. When you enter their space, radiating positive energy, and glowing gratitude, the atmosphere will shift. It will transform into the energy that attracts abundance, benefiting everyone around you.

Be specific on affirmations of gratitude. Be specific about what you're grateful for or what you're affirming. This specificity can enhance the emotional impact.

"I am thankful for my strong immune system that keeps me healthy and resilient."

There is no limit on abundance. Everything and anything you wish for or desire for your life is possible. Thing BIG! Say the things that you feel deep down in your soul. Keep speaking thankful affirmations until you can't think of anything else to say. You'll be surprised at how your thankful thoughts start to flow, beginning slowly and then picking up speed.

"I am thankful I read this book."

"I feel so lucky my life is always full of love and peace."

"I am excited to speak positivity over my life!"

You don't have to censor your words. Speak the loudest and most brave, out of this world, affirmations. Nothing is too big or too small. Use these processes to refine your affirmation practice and be thankful of every, single, thing in your life from the bees to the clouds, to the car you drive, and roads you drive on.

"I'm grateful for the sweet tea in my glass and the love in my heart."

YOUR. LIFE. WILL. CHANGE.

"I am thankful for the abundance I am receiving today."

"I appreciate contrast in my life to refine my wants and needs."

"I am so in love with my circle of friends and family."

"I am grateful for my health and strong body."

"Thank you for waking me up this morning."

"Thank you for this glorious day."

"Thank you for the blessings I see and the ones I've yet to receive."

"I am thankful for challenges that refine & strengthen me."

"I am capable of recognizing my blessings, big and small."

"I treasure peace & comfort that my environment offers me."

"I am grateful for the knowledge & wisdom shared with me by others."

MY AFFIRMATIONS WORKSHEET

"Let everything you say be good and helpful, so that your words will be an encouragement to those that hear them."

Ephesians 4:29

References

Newton-John, O. (1980). Magic [Song]. On Xanadu (Original Motion Picture Soundtrack). MCA Records.

Casting Crowns. (2003). Voice of Truth [Song]. On Casting Crowns. Beach Street Records.

Brooks, Garth. 1993. Callin' Baton Rouge. On In Pieces. Liberty Records.

Angelou, M. (1969). I know why the caged bird sings. Random House.

Bible versus:

The Holy Bible. (1982). New King James Version. Thomas Nelson.

The Holy Bible: New International Version. (2011). Zondervan.

About the Author

Angela was raised in a quaint town just outside of New Orleans, Louisiana. She built a life there until Hurricane Katrina claimed her home. In the aftermath, she relocated slightly north to Baton Rouge, Louisiana, where she now lives with her two dogs, Cooper and Deuce.

Following significant life changes, Angela shifted her focus to her writing career. She also launched several coaching businesses and uses her expertise to assist others in enhancing their eCommerce ventures, leveraging her extensive background in the field.

These days, Angela loves life with her two dogs and stays close to her children, along with cherishing moments with her new grandbaby.

Whether it's sipping sweet tea on the porch or finding joy in the everyday moments, she weaves her love for Southern simplicity and the magic of self-growth into everything she does.

You can reach Angela and learn more about her and her books at:

Email: angela@sweettalkbook.com

SweetTalkBook.com

Find us on all social channels: @SweetTalkBook

I can't wait to hear how this book changes your life!

Leave a comment on our social sites, send an email, or tagus in

your Sweet Talk experiences!